THE MAN WHO SH
LUCKY LUKE

SCRIPT, ARTWORK AND COLOURS
MATTHIEU BONHOMME

9th CINEBOOK
The 9th Art Publisher

To me, Lucky Luke is far more than an outstanding comic character created by a genius author. He's a traveling companion, a childhood friend – which made writing and drawing this book an immense pleasure. That is why I want to give special thanks to Francine de Bevere and publisher Lucky Comics for offering me the opportunity to go on this adventure.

Matthieu Bonhomme

Original title: L'homme qui tua Lucky Luke
Original edition: © Lucky Comics 2016 by Bonhomme
© Lucky Comics
www.lucky-luke.com
English translation: © 2022 Cinebook Ltd
Translator: Jerome Saincantin
Editor: Erica Olson Jeffrey
Lettering and text layout: Design Amorandi
Printed in Spain by EGEDSA
This edition first published in Great Britain in 2022 by
Cinebook Ltd
56 Beech Avenue
Canterbury, Kent
CT4 7TA
www.cinebook.com
A CIP catalogue record for this book
is available from the British Library
ISBN 978-1-80044-063-0

9th CINEBOOK
The 9th Art Publisher

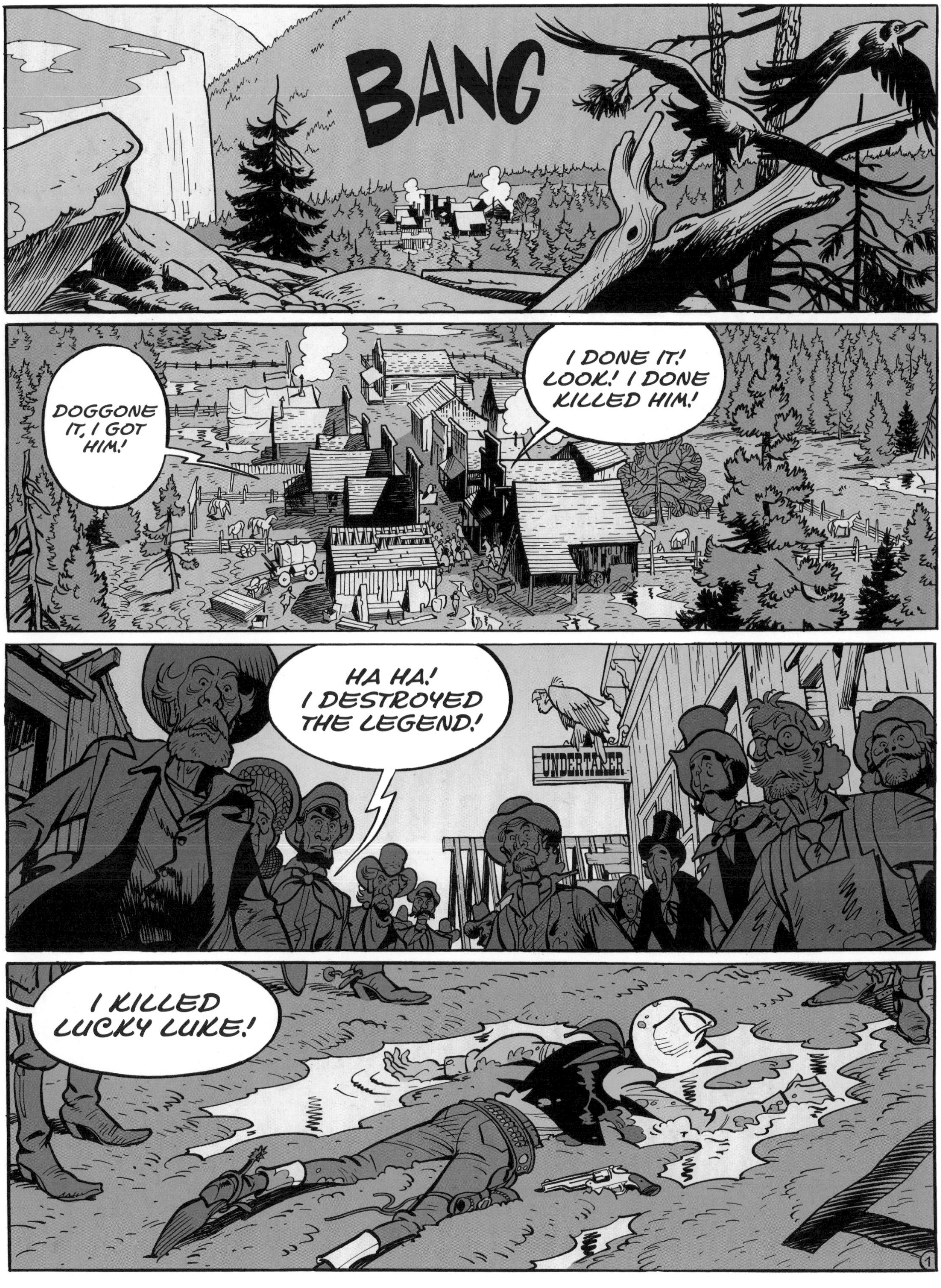
BANG
DOGGONE IT, I GOT HIM!
I DONE IT! LOOK! I DONE KILLED HIM!
HA HA! I DESTROYED THE LEGEND!
UNDERTAKER
I KILLED LUCKY LUKE!

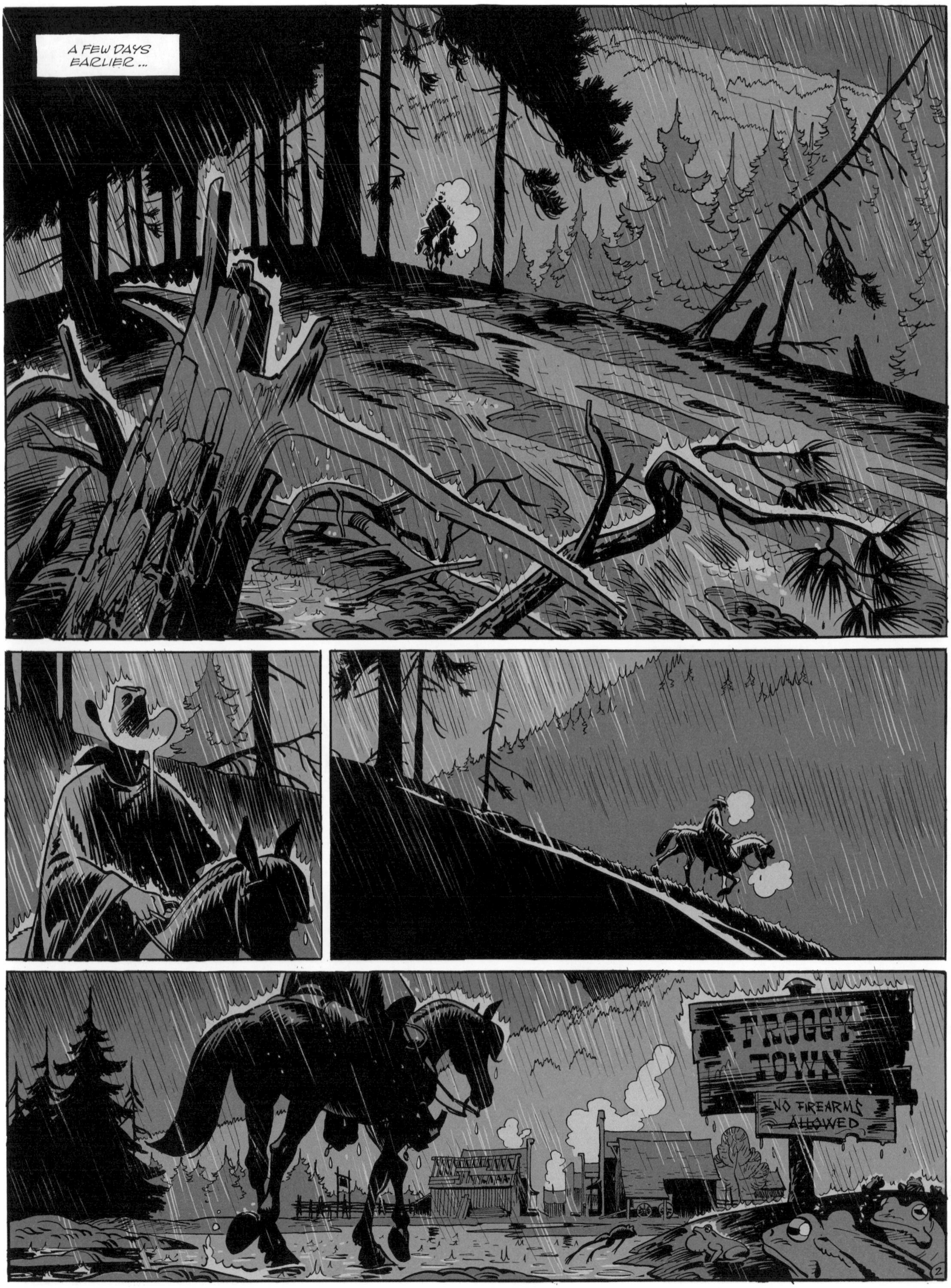
A FEW DAYS EARLIER ...
FROGGY TOWN
NO FIREARMS ALLOWED

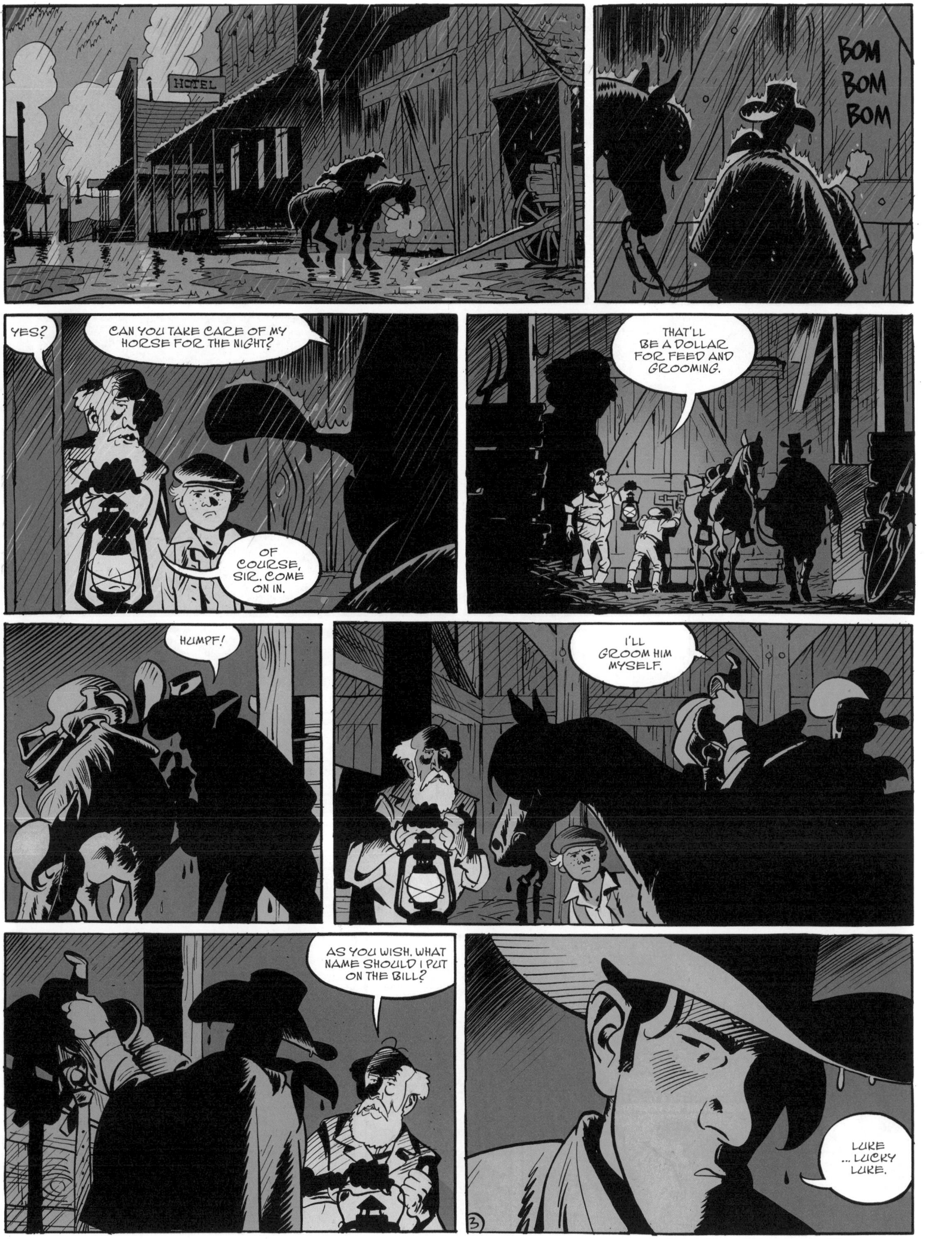
BOM
BOM
BOM
YES?
CAN YOU TAKE CARE OF MY HORSE FOR THE NIGHT?
OF COURSE, SIR. COME ON IN.
THAT'LL BE A DOLLAR FOR FEED AND GROOMING.
HUMPF!
I'LL GROOM HIM MYSELF.
AS YOU WISH. WHAT NAME SHOULD I PUT ON THE BILL?
LUKE ...LUCKY LUKE.

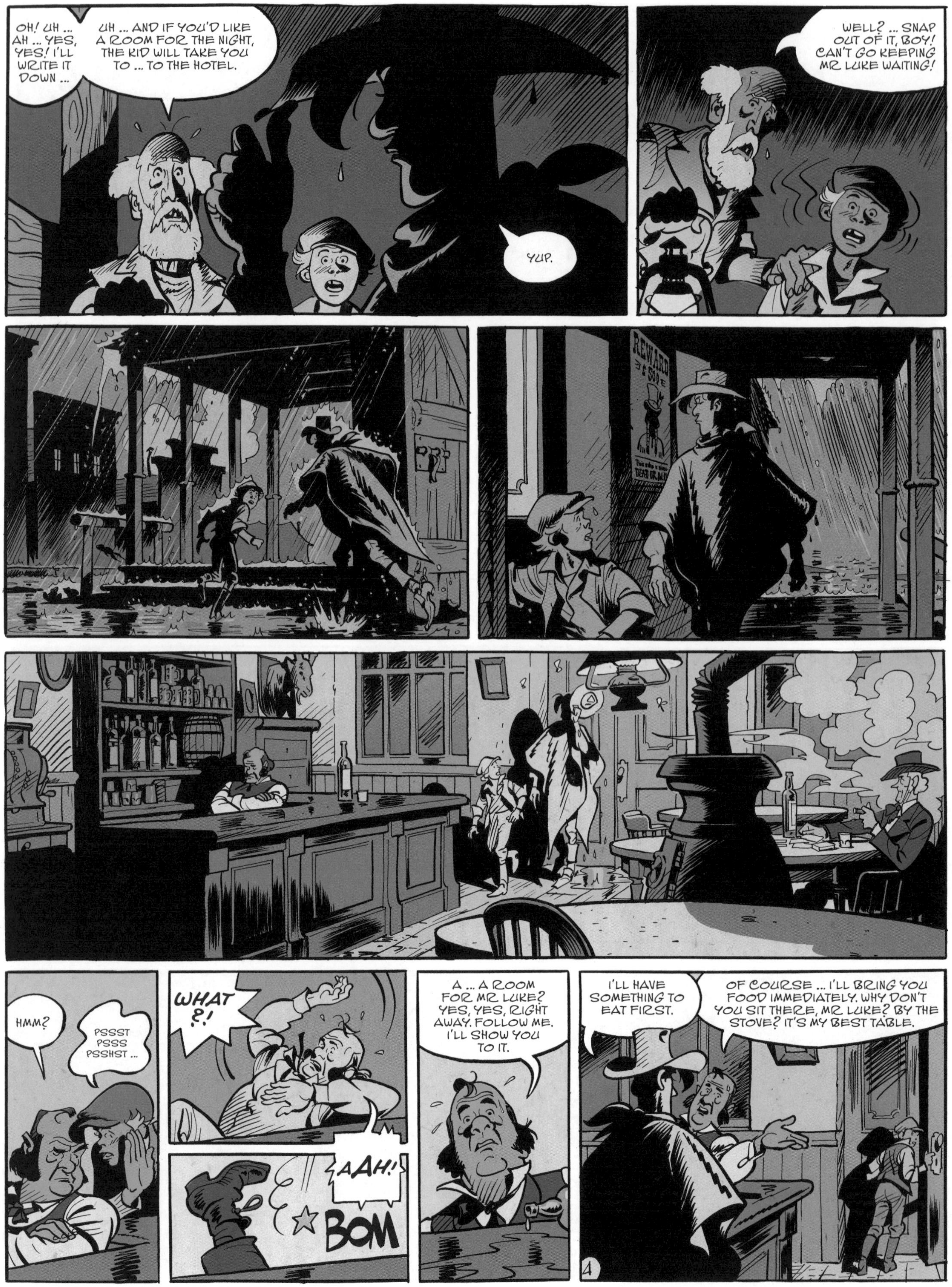
OH! UH ... AH ... YES, YES! I'LL WRITE IT DOWN ...
UH ... AND IF YOU'D LIKE A ROOM FOR THE NIGHT, THE KID WILL TAKE YOU TO ... TO THE HOTEL.
YUP.
WELL? ... SNAP OUT OF IT, BOY! CAN'T GO KEEPING MR LUKE WAITING!
REWARD
HMM?
PSSST PSSS PSSHST ...
WHAT ?!
AAH!
BOM
A ... A ROOM FOR MR LUKE? YES, YES, RIGHT AWAY. FOLLOW ME. I'LL SHOW YOU TO IT.
I'LL HAVE SOMETHING TO EAT FIRST.
OF COURSE ... I'LL BRING YOU FOOD IMMEDIATELY. WHY DON'T YOU SIT THERE, MR LUKE? BY THE STOVE? IT'S MY BEST TABLE.
4

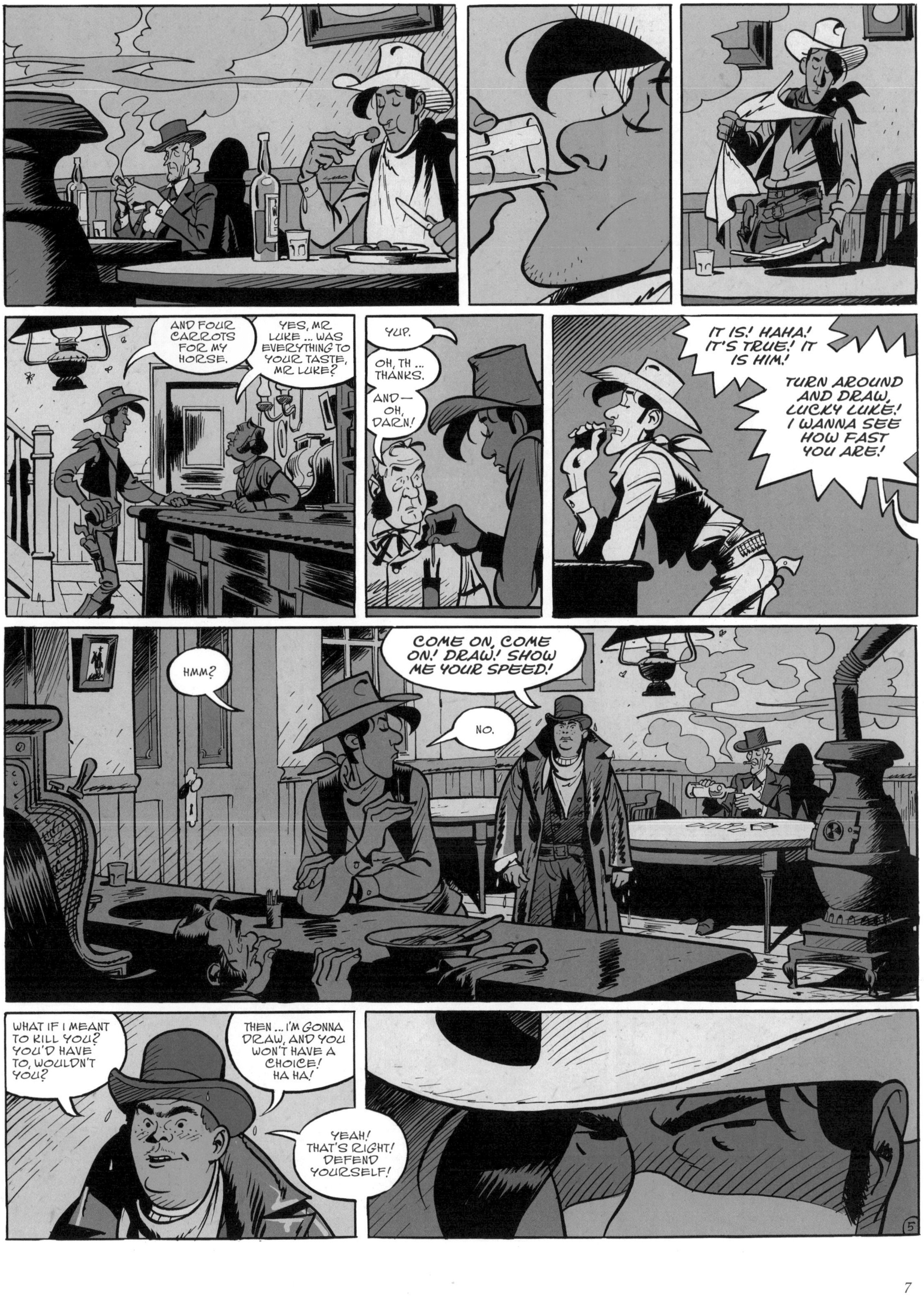
AND FOUR CARROTS FOR MY HORSE.
YES, MR LUKE ... WAS EVERYTHING TO YOUR TASTE, MR LUKE?
YUP.
OH, TH ... THANKS.
AND— OH, DARN!
IT IS! HAHA! IT'S TRUE! IT IS HIM!
TURN AROUND AND DRAW, LUCKY LUKE! I WANNA SEE HOW FAST YOU ARE!
HMM?
COME ON, COME ON! DRAW! SHOW ME YOUR SPEED!
NO.
WHAT IF I MEANT TO KILL YOU? YOU'D HAVE TO, WOULDN'T YOU?
THEN ... I'M GONNA DRAW, AND YOU WON'T HAVE A CHOICE! HA HA!
YEAH! THAT'S RIGHT! DEFEND YOURSELF!
5

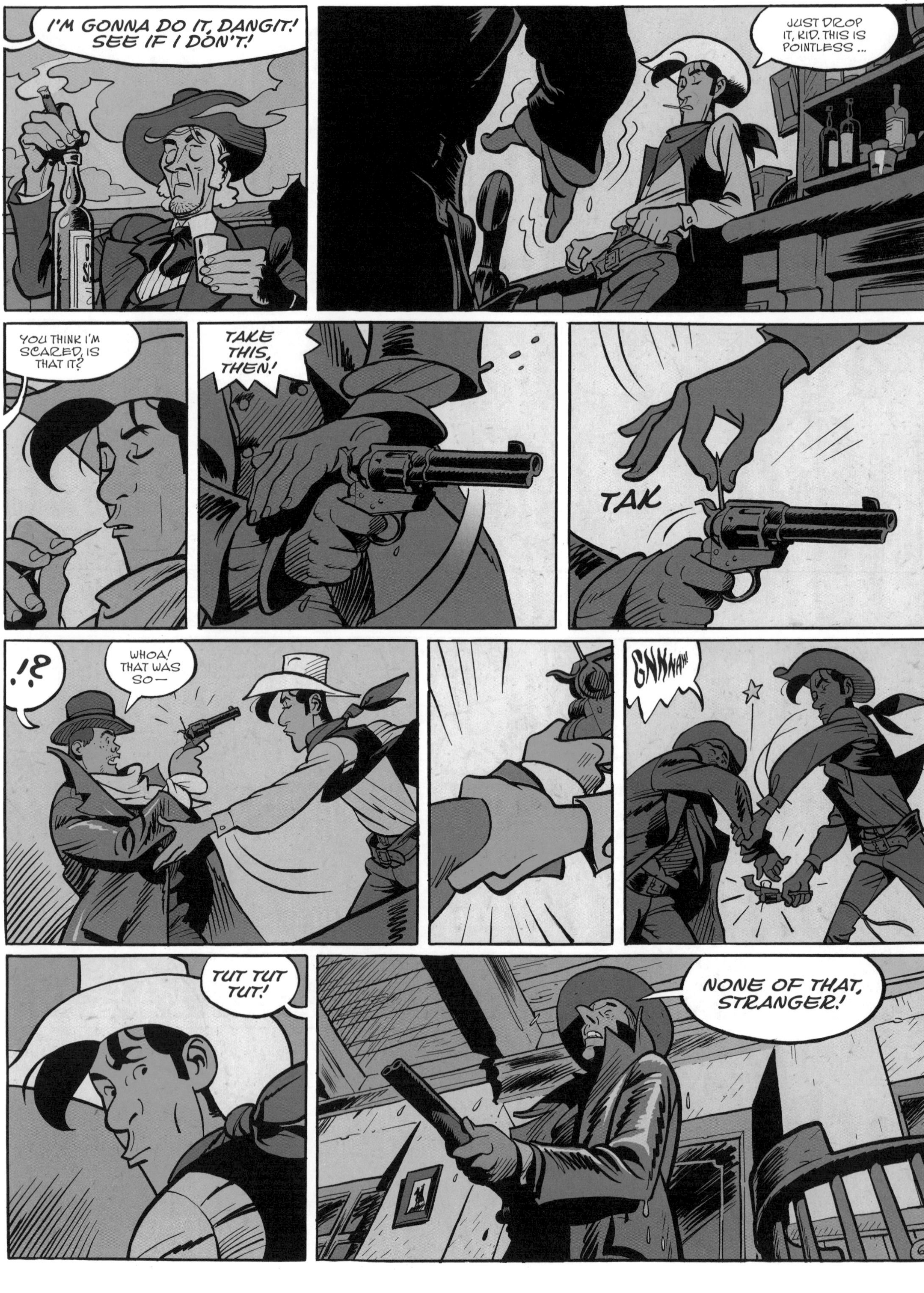
I'M GONNA DO IT, DANGIT! SEE IF I DON'T!
JUST DROP IT, KID. THIS IS POINTLESS ...
YOU THINK I'M SCARED, IS THAT IT?
TAKE THIS, THEN!
TAK
!?
WHOA! THAT WAS SO—
GNNNAH!
TUT TUT TUT!
NONE OF THAT, STRANGER!
6

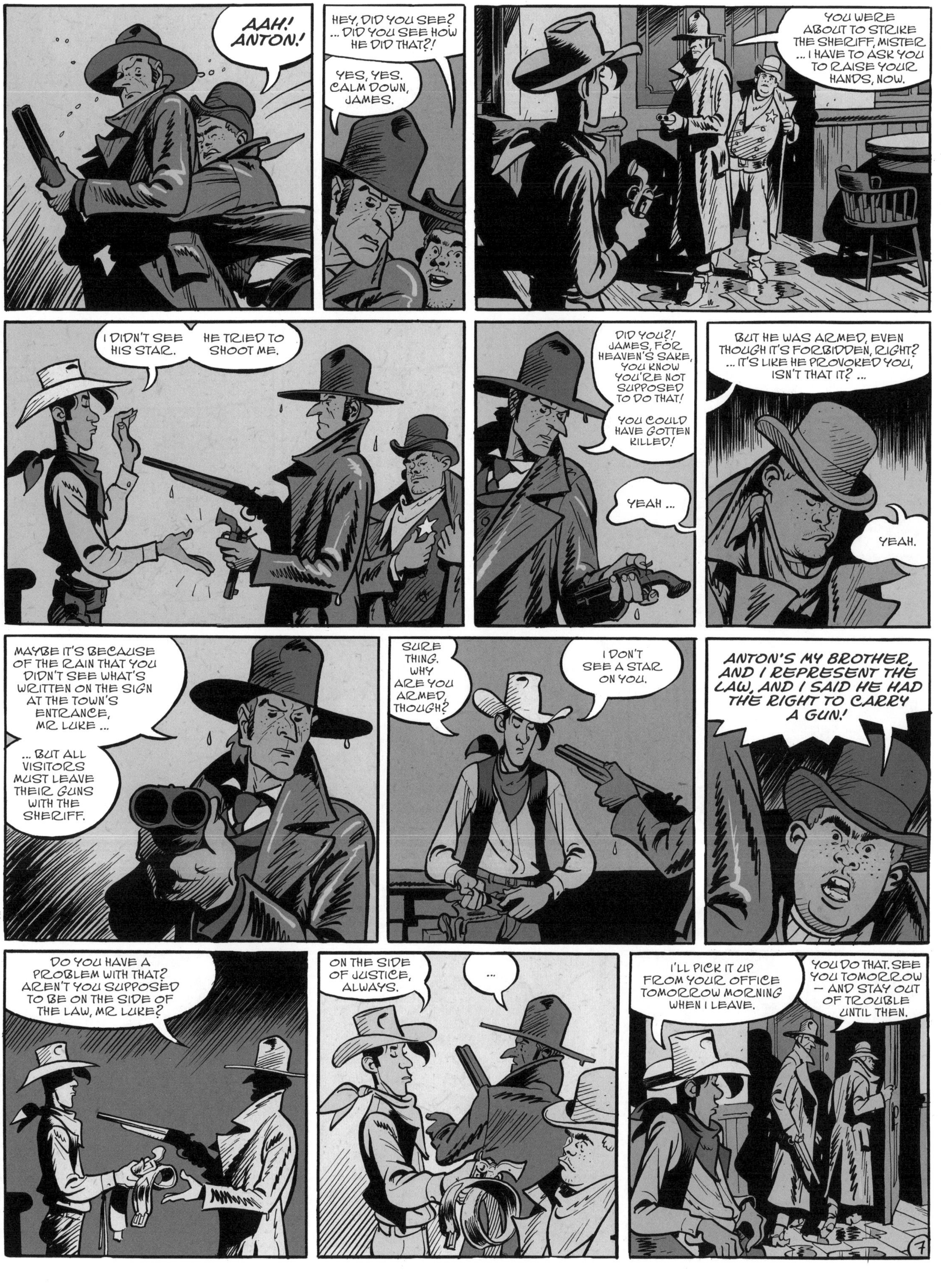
AAH! ANTON!
HEY, DID YOU SEE? ... DID YOU SEE HOW HE DID THAT?!
YES, YES. CALM DOWN, JAMES.
YOU WERE ABOUT TO STRIKE THE SHERIFF, MISTER ... I HAVE TO ASK YOU TO RAISE YOUR HANDS, NOW.
I DIDN'T SEE HIS STAR.
HE TRIED TO SHOOT ME.
DID YOU?! JAMES, FOR HEAVEN'S SAKE, YOU KNOW YOU'RE NOT SUPPOSED TO DO THAT!
YOU COULD HAVE GOTTEN KILLED!
YEAH ...
BUT HE WAS ARMED, EVEN THOUGH IT'S FORBIDDEN, RIGHT? ... IT'S LIKE HE PROVOKED YOU, ISN'T THAT IT? ...
YEAH.
MAYBE IT'S BECAUSE OF THE RAIN THAT YOU DIDN'T SEE WHAT'S WRITTEN ON THE SIGN AT THE TOWN'S ENTRANCE, MR LUKE ...
... BUT ALL VISITORS MUST LEAVE THEIR GUNS WITH THE SHERIFF.
SURE THING. WHY ARE YOU ARMED, THOUGH?
I DON'T SEE A STAR ON YOU.
ANTON'S MY BROTHER, AND I REPRESENT THE LAW, AND I SAID HE HAD THE RIGHT TO CARRY A GUN!
DO YOU HAVE A PROBLEM WITH THAT? AREN'T YOU SUPPOSED TO BE ON THE SIDE OF THE LAW, MR LUKE?
ON THE SIDE OF JUSTICE, ALWAYS.
...
I'LL PICK IT UP FROM YOUR OFFICE TOMORROW MORNING WHEN I LEAVE.
YOU DO THAT. SEE YOU TOMORROW – AND STAY OUT OF TROUBLE UNTIL THEN.
7

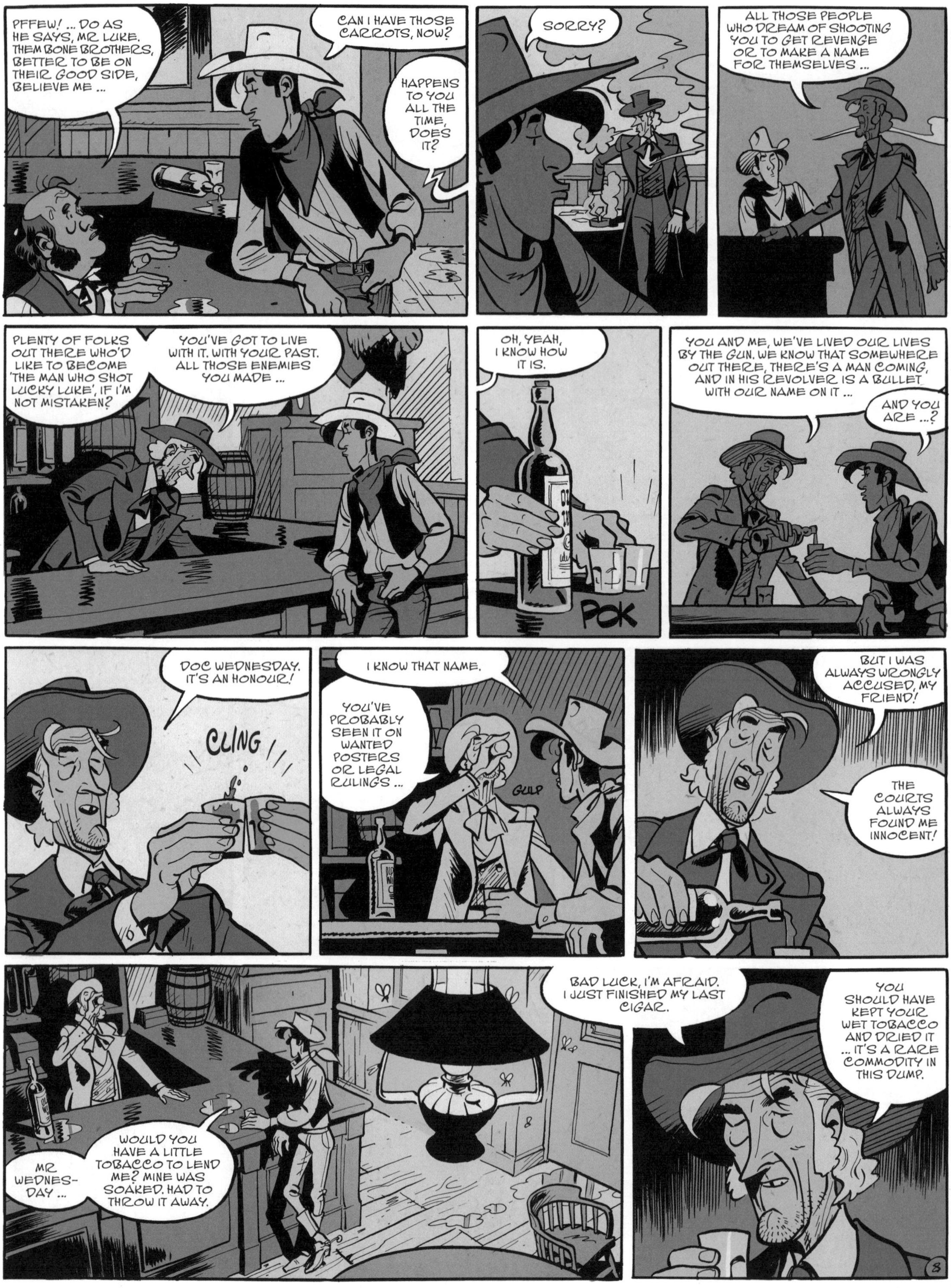
PFFEW! ... DO AS HE SAYS, MR LUKE. THEM BONE BROTHERS, BETTER TO BE ON THEIR GOOD SIDE, BELIEVE ME ...
CAN I HAVE THOSE CARROTS, NOW?
HAPPENS TO YOU ALL THE TIME, DOES IT?
SORRY?
ALL THOSE PEOPLE WHO DREAM OF SHOOTING YOU TO GET REVENGE OR TO MAKE A NAME FOR THEMSELVES ...
PLENTY OF FOLKS OUT THERE WHO'D LIKE TO BECOME 'THE MAN WHO SHOT LUCKY LUKE', IF I'M NOT MISTAKEN?
YOU'VE GOT TO LIVE WITH IT. WITH YOUR PAST. ALL THOSE ENEMIES YOU MADE ...
OH, YEAH, I KNOW HOW IT IS.
POK
YOU AND ME, WE'VE LIVED OUR LIVES BY THE GUN. WE KNOW THAT SOMEWHERE OUT THERE, THERE'S A MAN COMING, AND IN HIS REVOLVER IS A BULLET WITH OUR NAME ON IT ...
AND YOU ARE ...?
DOC WEDNESDAY. IT'S AN HONOUR!
CLING
I KNOW THAT NAME.
YOU'VE PROBABLY SEEN IT ON WANTED POSTERS OR LEGAL RULINGS ...
GULP
BUT I WAS ALWAYS WRONGLY ACCUSED, MY FRIEND!
THE COURTS ALWAYS FOUND ME INNOCENT!
MR WEDNES-DAY ...
WOULD YOU HAVE A LITTLE TOBACCO TO LEND ME? MINE WAS SOAKED. HAD TO THROW IT AWAY.
BAD LUCK, I'M AFRAID. I JUST FINISHED MY LAST CIGAR.
YOU SHOULD HAVE KEPT YOUR WET TOBACCO AND DRIED IT ... IT'S A RARE COMMODITY IN THIS DUMP.
8

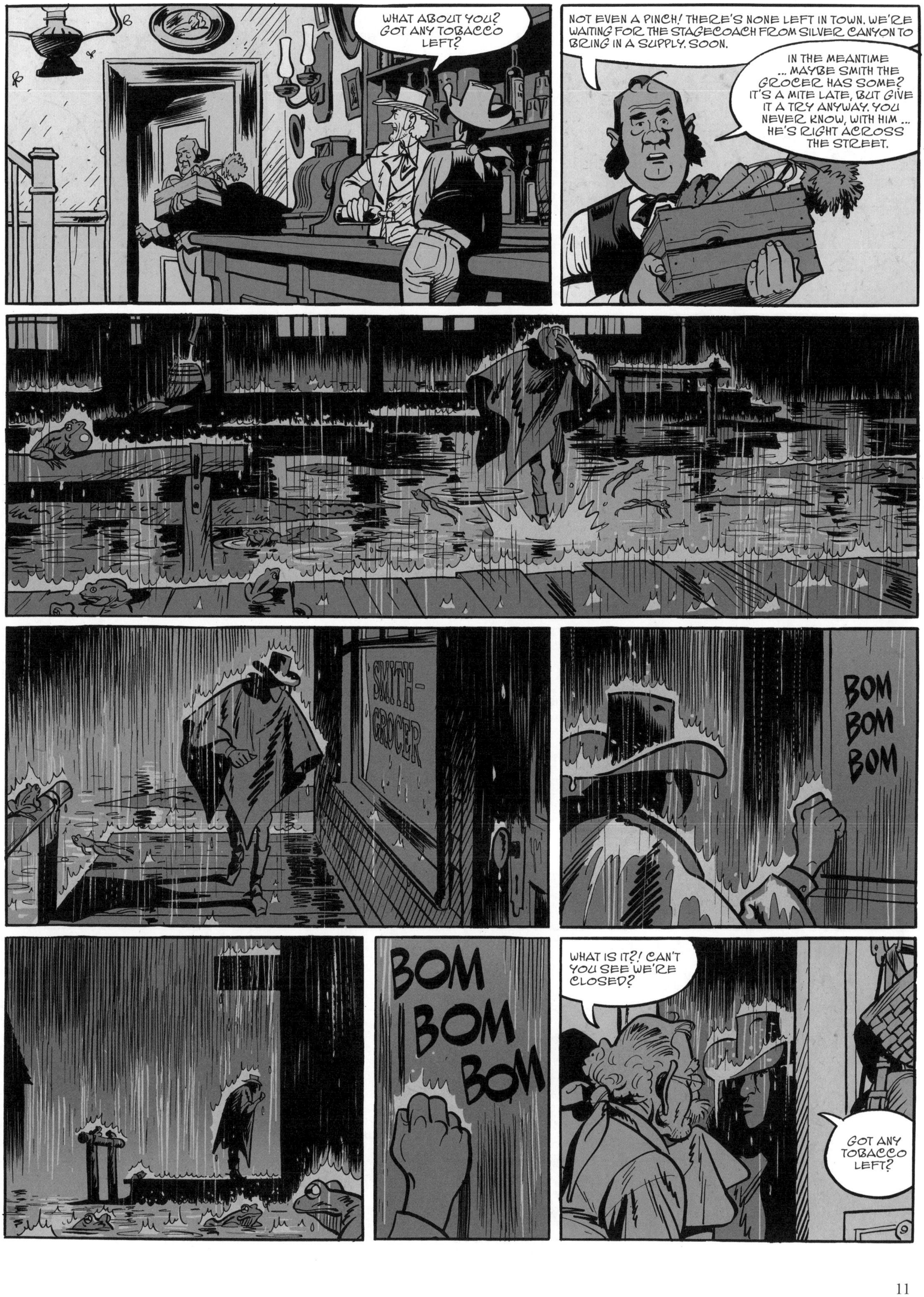
WHAT ABOUT YOU? GOT ANY TOBACCO LEFT?
NOT EVEN A PINCH! THERE'S NONE LEFT IN TOWN. WE'RE WAITING FOR THE STAGECOACH FROM SILVER CANYON TO BRING IN A SUPPLY. SOON.
IN THE MEANTIME ... MAYBE SMITH THE GROCER HAS SOME? IT'S A MITE LATE, BUT GIVE IT A TRY ANYWAY. YOU NEVER KNOW, WITH HIM ... HE'S RIGHT ACROSS THE STREET.
SMITH-GROCER
BOM BOM BOM
BOM BOM BOM
WHAT IS IT?! CAN'T YOU SEE WE'RE CLOSED?
GOT ANY TOBACCO LEFT?

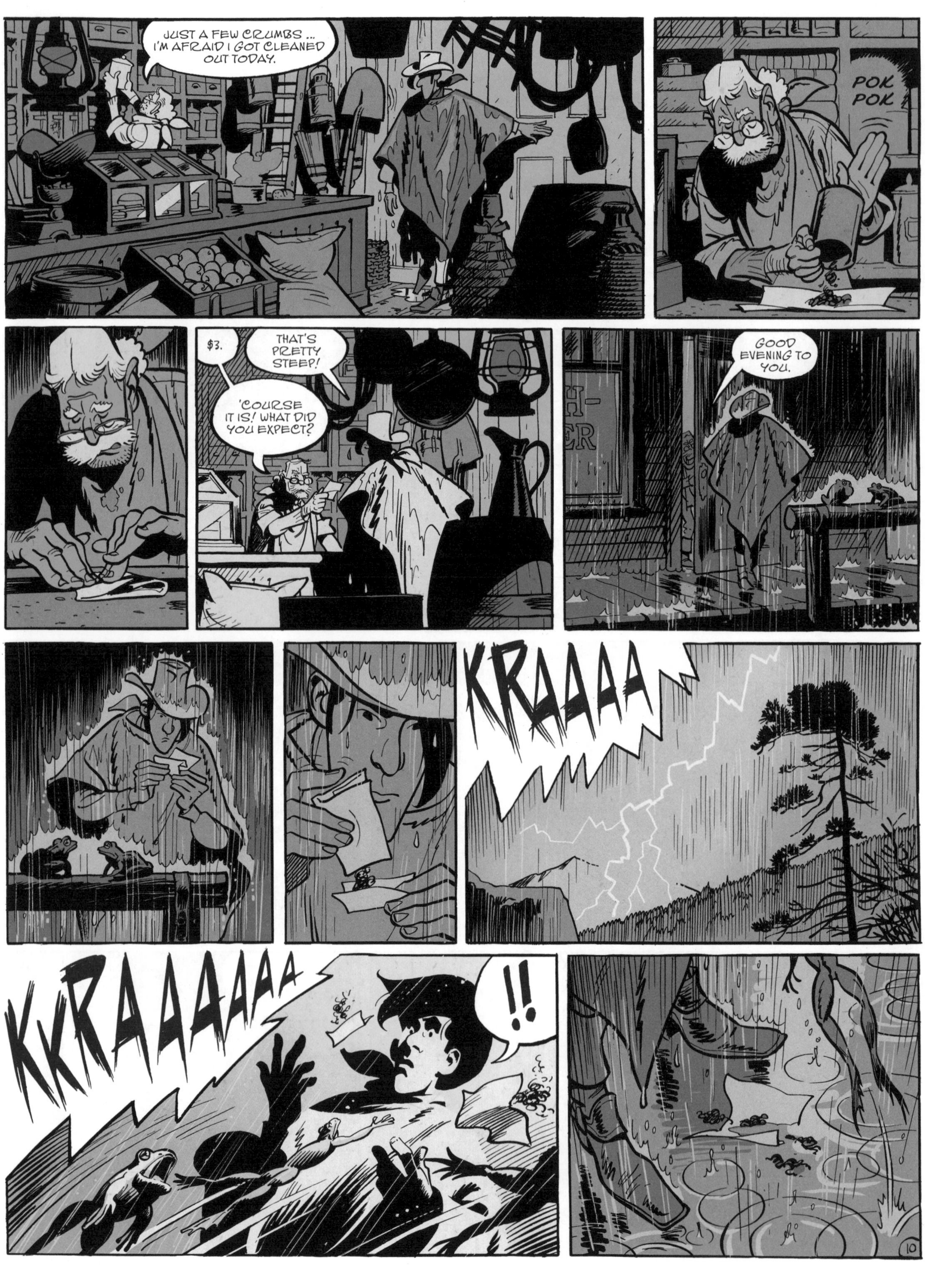
JUST A FEW CRUMBS ... I'M AFRAID I GOT CLEANED OUT TODAY.
POK POK
$3.
THAT'S PRETTY STEEP!
'COURSE IT IS! WHAT DID YOU EXPECT?
GOOD EVENING TO YOU.
KRAAAA
KKRAAAAAAA
!!

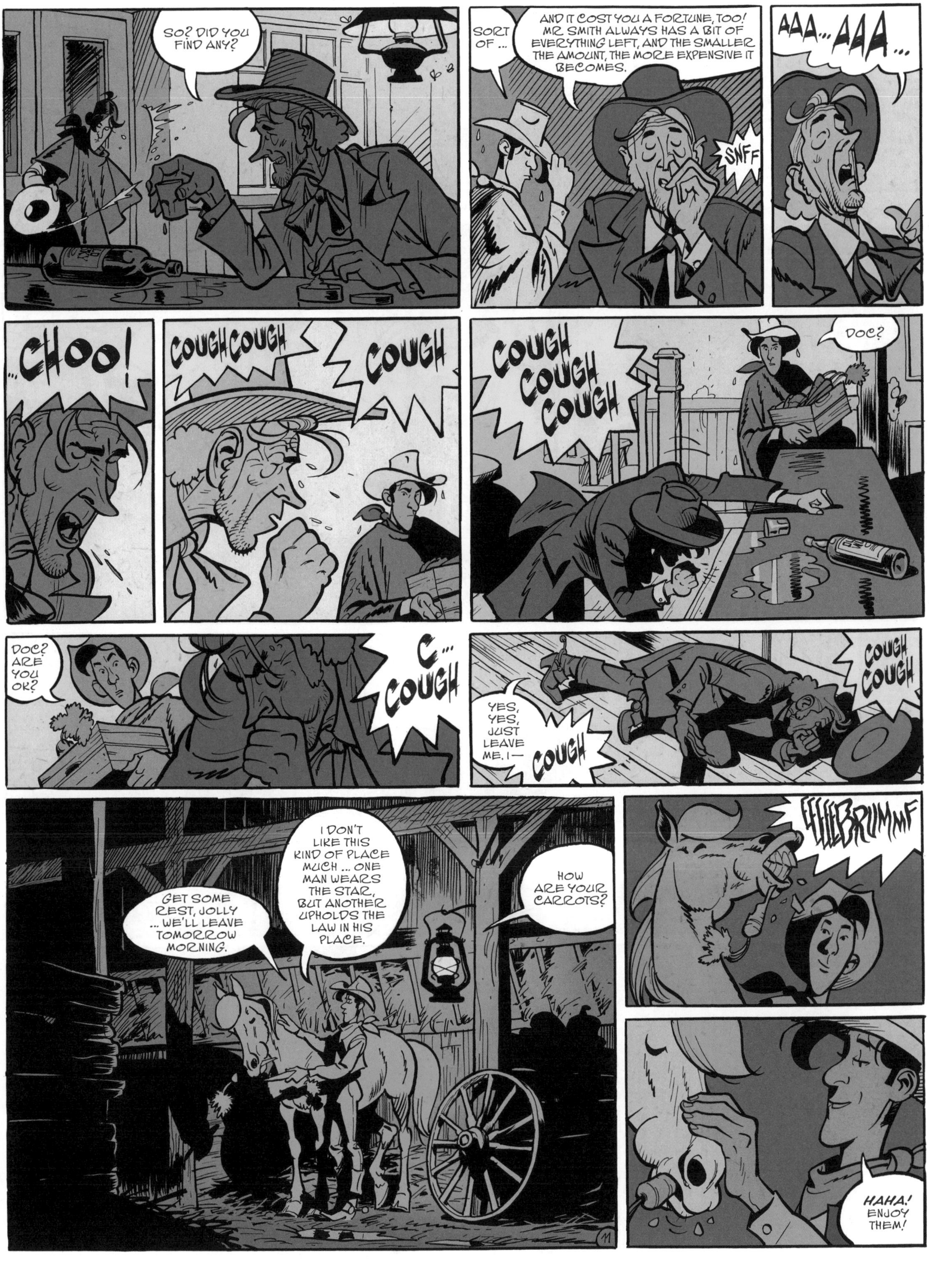
SO? DID YOU FIND ANY?
SORT OF ...
AND IT COST YOU A FORTUNE, TOO! MR SMITH ALWAYS HAS A BIT OF EVERYTHING LEFT, AND THE SMALLER THE AMOUNT, THE MORE EXPENSIVE IT BECOMES.
SNFF
AAA... AAA...
...CHOO!
COUGH COUGH
COUGH
COUGH COUGH COUGH
DOC?
DOC? ARE YOU OK?
C... COUGH
COUGH COUGH
YES, YES, JUST LEAVE ME. I—
COUGH
GET SOME REST, JOLLY ... WE'LL LEAVE TOMORROW MORNING.
I DON'T LIKE THIS KIND OF PLACE MUCH ... ONE MAN WEARS THE STAR, BUT ANOTHER UPHOLDS THE LAW IN HIS PLACE.
HOW ARE YOUR CARROTS?
EEEEBRUMMF
HAHA! ENJOY THEM!

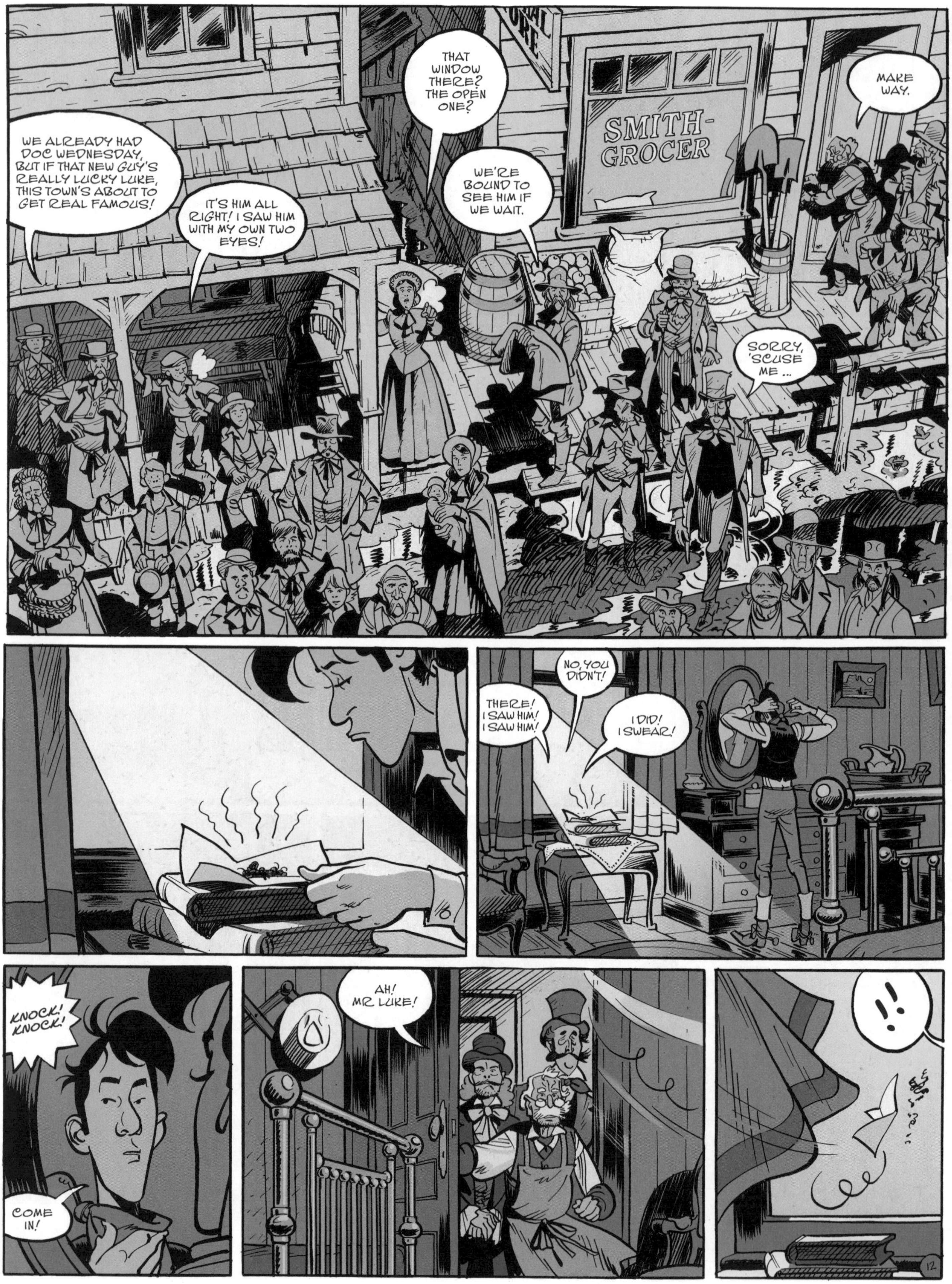
WE ALREADY HAD DOC WEDNESDAY, BUT IF THAT NEW GUY'S REALLY LUCKY LUKE, THIS TOWN'S ABOUT TO GET REAL FAMOUS!
IT'S HIM ALL RIGHT! I SAW HIM WITH MY OWN TWO EYES!
THAT WINDOW THERE? THE OPEN ONE?
WE'RE BOUND TO SEE HIM IF WE WAIT.
SMITH-GROCER
MAKE WAY.
SORRY, 'SCUSE ME ...
THERE! I SAW HIM! I SAW HIM!
NO, YOU DIDN'T!
I DID! I SWEAR!
KNOCK! KNOCK!
COME IN!
AH! MR LUKE!
!!

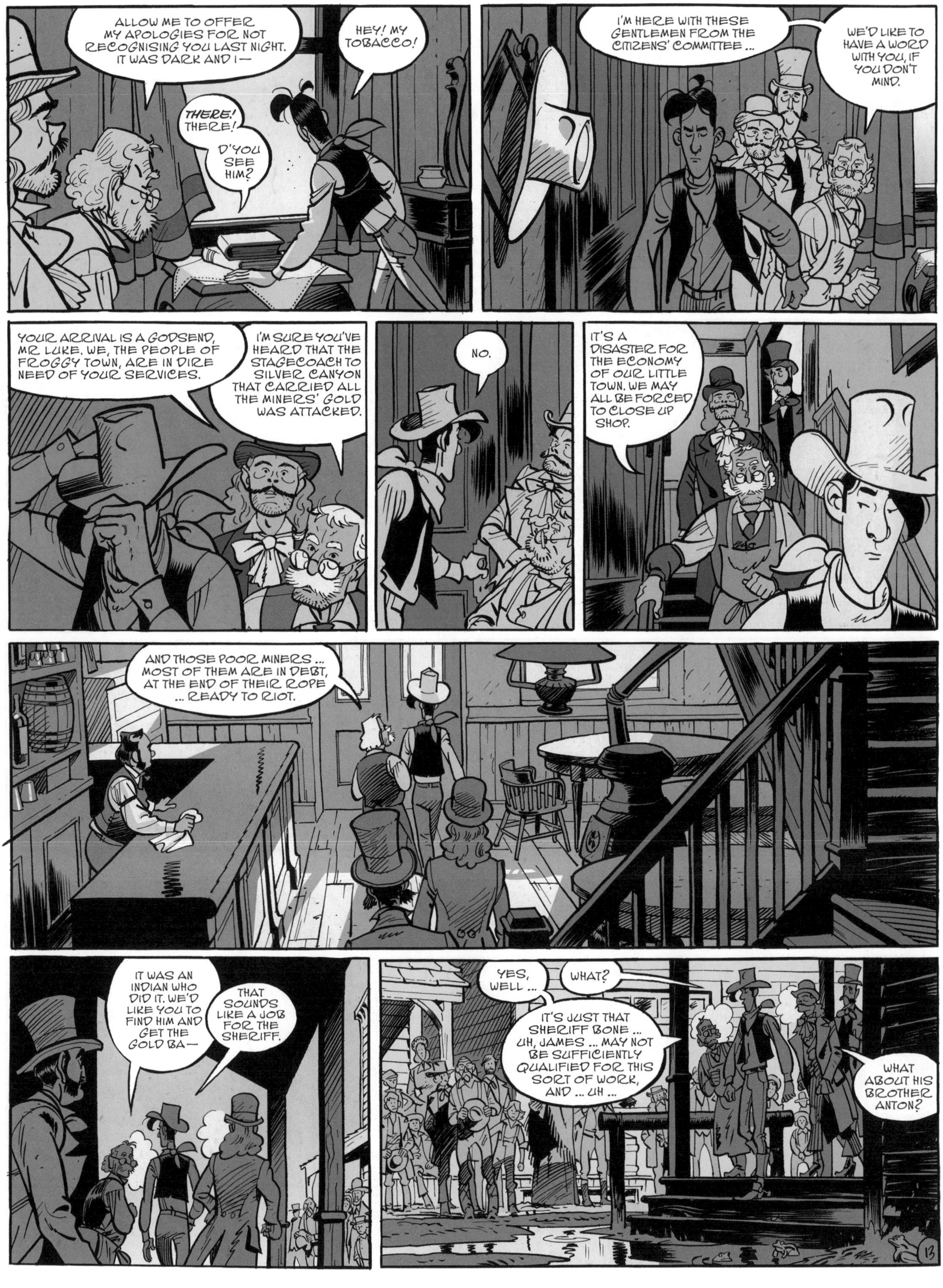
ALLOW ME TO OFFER MY APOLOGIES FOR NOT RECOGNISING YOU LAST NIGHT. IT WAS DARK AND I—
HEY! MY TOBACCO!
THERE! THERE!
D'YOU SEE HIM?
I'M HERE WITH THESE GENTLEMEN FROM THE CITIZENS' COMMITTEE ...
WE'D LIKE TO HAVE A WORD WITH YOU, IF YOU DON'T MIND.
YOUR ARRIVAL IS A GODSEND, MR LUKE. WE, THE PEOPLE OF FROGGY TOWN, ARE IN DIRE NEED OF YOUR SERVICES.
I'M SURE YOU'VE HEARD THAT THE STAGECOACH TO SILVER CANYON THAT CARRIED ALL THE MINERS' GOLD WAS ATTACKED.
NO.
IT'S A DISASTER FOR THE ECONOMY OF OUR LITTLE TOWN. WE MAY ALL BE FORCED TO CLOSE UP SHOP.
AND THOSE POOR MINERS ... MOST OF THEM ARE IN DEBT, AT THE END OF THEIR ROPE ... READY TO RIOT.
IT WAS AN INDIAN WHO DID IT. WE'D LIKE YOU TO FIND HIM AND GET THE GOLD BA—
THAT SOUNDS LIKE A JOB FOR THE SHERIFF.
YES, WELL ...
WHAT?
IT'S JUST THAT SHERIFF BONE ... UH, JAMES ... MAY NOT BE SUFFICIENTLY QUALIFIED FOR THIS SORT OF WORK, AND ... UH ...
WHAT ABOUT HIS BROTHER ANTON?
13

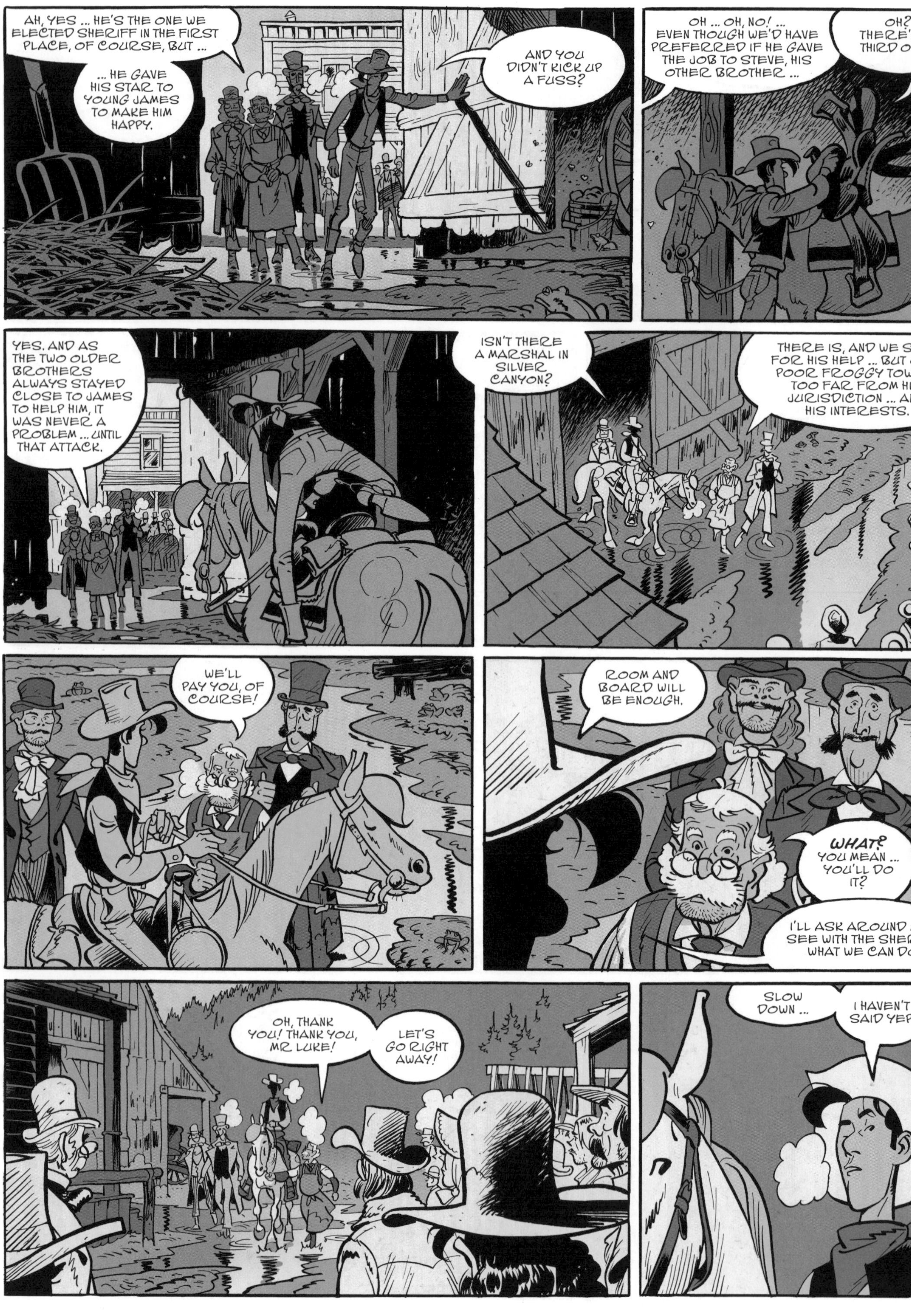

AH, YES ... HE'S THE ONE WE ELECTED SHERIFF IN THE FIRST PLACE, OF COURSE, BUT ...
... HE GAVE HIS STAR TO YOUNG JAMES TO MAKE HIM HAPPY.
AND YOU DIDN'T KICK UP A FUSS?
OH ... OH, NO! ... EVEN THOUGH WE'D HAVE PREFERRED IF HE GAVE THE JOB TO STEVE, HIS OTHER BROTHER ...
OH? THERE'S A THIRD ONE?
YES. AND AS THE TWO OLDER BROTHERS ALWAYS STAYED CLOSE TO JAMES TO HELP HIM, IT WAS NEVER A PROBLEM ... UNTIL THAT ATTACK.
ISN'T THERE A MARSHAL IN SILVER CANYON?
THERE IS, AND WE SENT FOR HIS HELP ... BUT OUR POOR FROGGY TOWN IS TOO FAR FROM HIS JURISDICTION ... AND HIS INTERESTS.
WE'LL PAY YOU, OF COURSE!
ROOM AND BOARD WILL BE ENOUGH.
WHAT? YOU MEAN ... YOU'LL DO IT?
I'LL ASK AROUND AND SEE WITH THE SHERIFF WHAT WE CAN DO.
OH, THANK YOU! THANK YOU, MR LUKE!
LET'S GO RIGHT AWAY!
SLOW DOWN ...
I HAVEN'T SAID YEP.
14

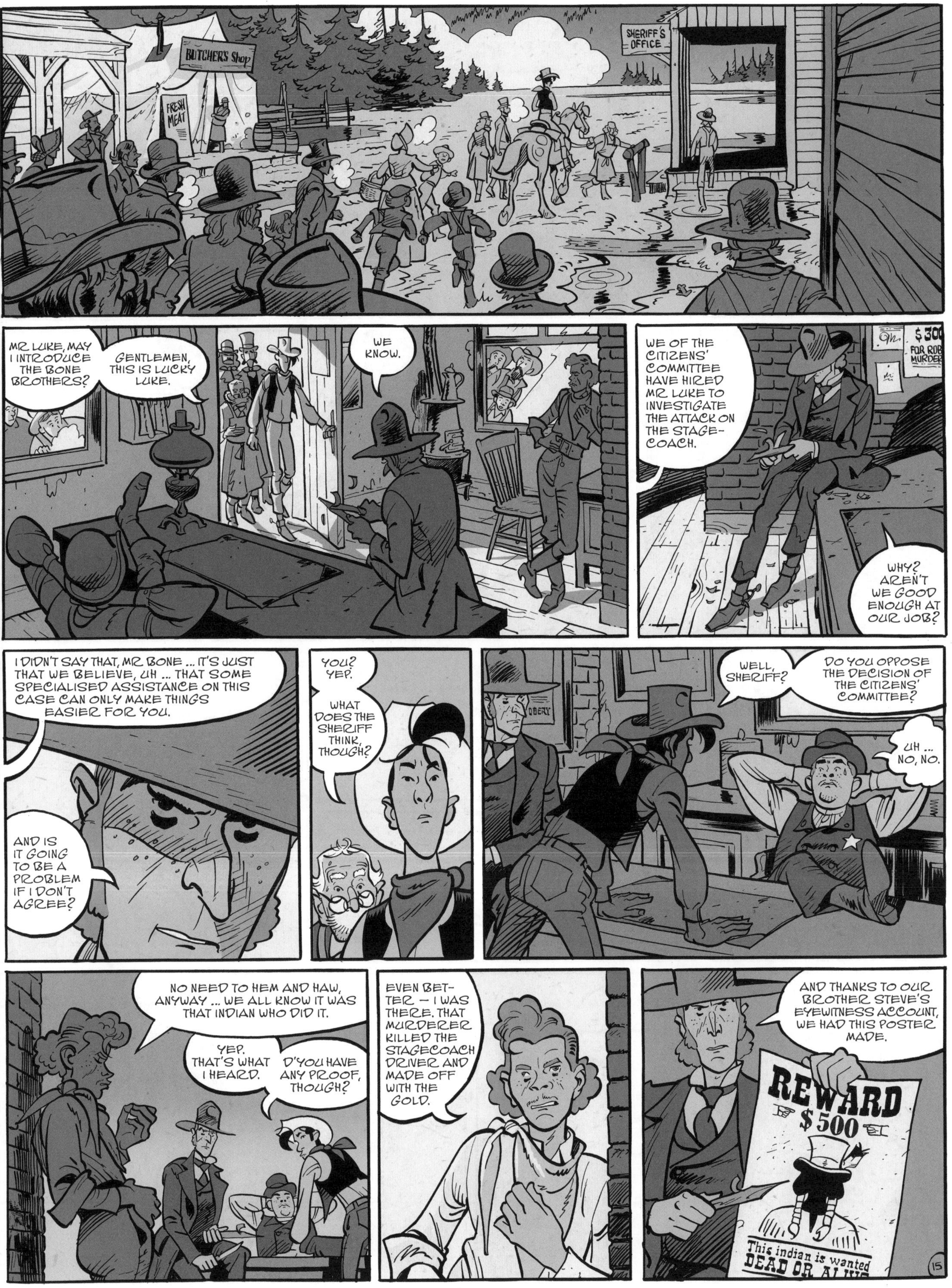
BUTCHER'S Shop
FRESH MEAT
SHERIFF'S OFFICE
MR LUKE, MAY I INTRODUCE THE BONE BROTHERS?
GENTLEMEN, THIS IS LUCKY LUKE.
WE KNOW.
WE OF THE CITIZENS' COMMITTEE HAVE HIRED MR LUKE TO INVESTIGATE THE ATTACK ON THE STAGE-COACH.
WHY? AREN'T WE GOOD ENOUGH AT OUR JOB?
I DIDN'T SAY THAT, MR BONE ... IT'S JUST THAT WE BELIEVE, UH ... THAT SOME SPECIALISED ASSISTANCE ON THIS CASE CAN ONLY MAKE THINGS EASIER FOR YOU.
AND IS IT GOING TO BE A PROBLEM IF I DON'T AGREE?
YOU? YEP.
WHAT DOES THE SHERIFF THINK, THOUGH?
WELL, SHERIFF?
DO YOU OPPOSE THE DECISION OF THE CITIZENS' COMMITTEE?
UH ... NO, NO.
NO NEED TO HEM AND HAW, ANYWAY ... WE ALL KNOW IT WAS THAT INDIAN WHO DID IT.
YEP. THAT'S WHAT I HEARD.
D'YOU HAVE ANY PROOF, THOUGH?
EVEN BET-TER – I WAS THERE. THAT MURDERER KILLED THE STAGECOACH DRIVER AND MADE OFF WITH THE GOLD.
AND THANKS TO OUR BROTHER STEVE'S EYEWITNESS ACCOUNT, WE HAD THIS POSTER MADE.
REWARD
$500
This indian is wanted
15

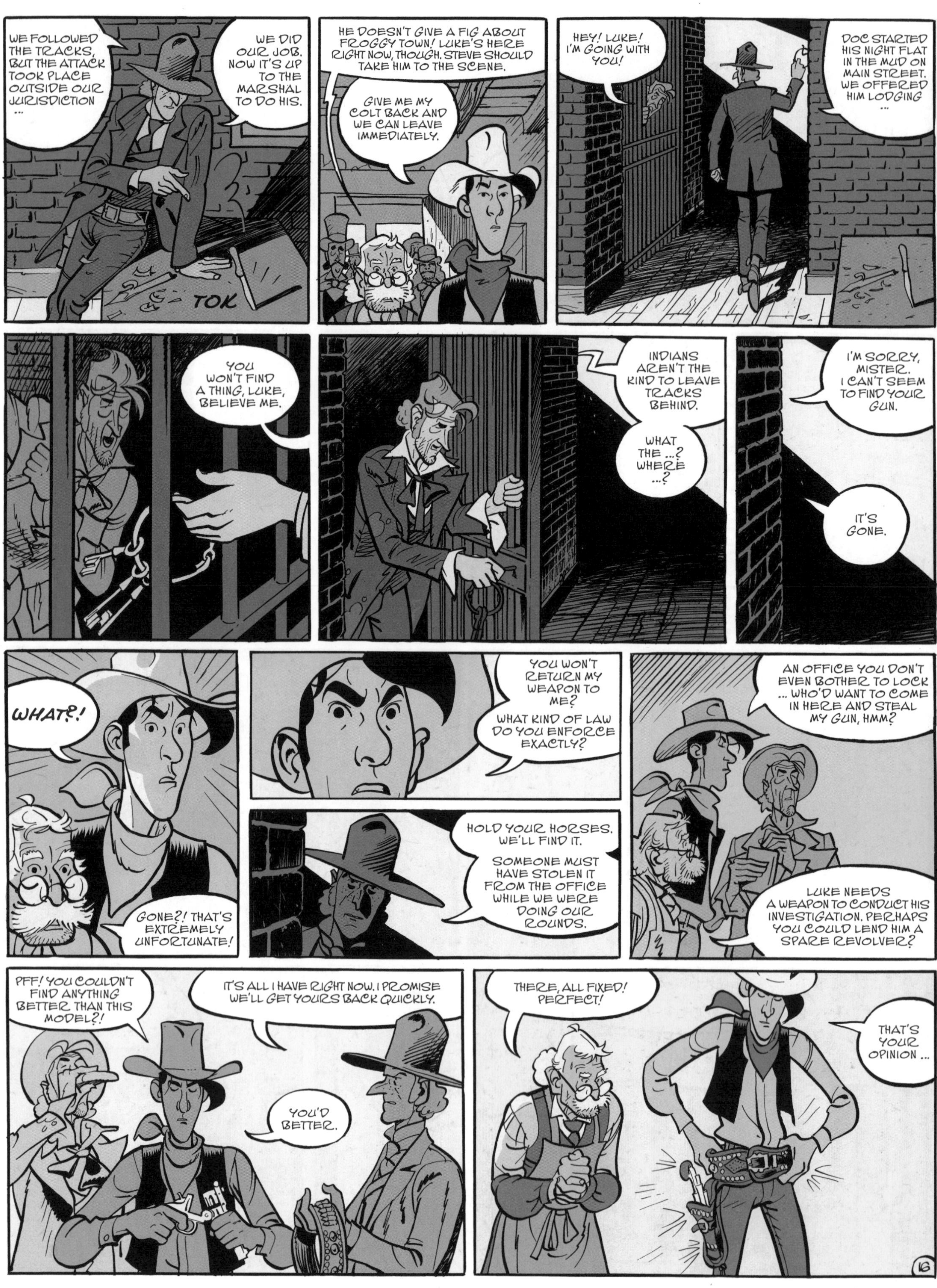

WE FOLLOWED THE TRACKS, BUT THE ATTACK TOOK PLACE OUTSIDE OUR JURISDICTION ...
WE DID OUR JOB. NOW IT'S UP TO THE MARSHAL TO DO HIS.
TOK
HE DOESN'T GIVE A FIG ABOUT FROGGY TOWN! LUKE'S HERE RIGHT NOW, THOUGH. STEVE SHOULD TAKE HIM TO THE SCENE.
GIVE ME MY COLT BACK AND WE CAN LEAVE IMMEDIATELY.
HEY! LUKE! I'M GOING WITH YOU!
DOC STARTED HIS NIGHT FLAT IN THE MUD ON MAIN STREET. WE OFFERED HIM LODGING ...
YOU WON'T FIND A THING, LUKE, BELIEVE ME.
INDIANS AREN'T THE KIND TO LEAVE TRACKS BEHIND.
WHAT THE ...? WHERE ...?
I'M SORRY, MISTER. I CAN'T SEEM TO FIND YOUR GUN.
IT'S GONE.
WHAT?!
GONE?! THAT'S EXTREMELY UNFORTUNATE!
YOU WON'T RETURN MY WEAPON TO ME?
WHAT KIND OF LAW DO YOU ENFORCE EXACTLY?
HOLD YOUR HORSES. WE'LL FIND IT.
SOMEONE MUST HAVE STOLEN IT FROM THE OFFICE WHILE WE WERE DOING OUR ROUNDS.
AN OFFICE YOU DON'T EVEN BOTHER TO LOCK ... WHO'D WANT TO COME IN HERE AND STEAL MY GUN, HMM?
LUKE NEEDS A WEAPON TO CONDUCT HIS INVESTIGATION. PERHAPS YOU COULD LEND HIM A SPARE REVOLVER?
PFF! YOU COULDN'T FIND ANYTHING BETTER THAN THIS MODEL?!
IT'S ALL I HAVE RIGHT NOW. I PROMISE WE'LL GET YOURS BACK QUICKLY.
YOU'D BETTER.
THERE, ALL FIXED! PERFECT!
THAT'S YOUR OPINION ...
16

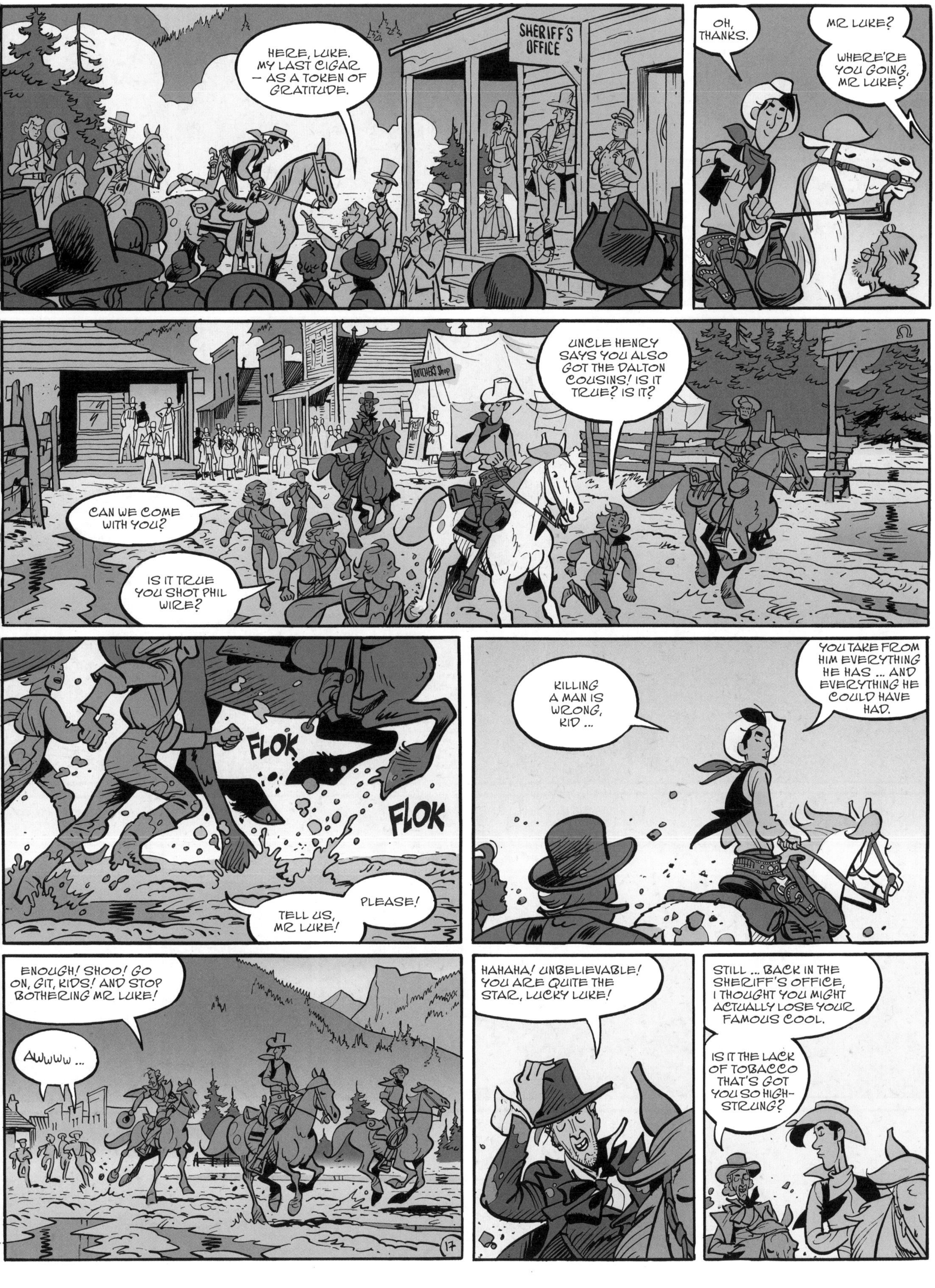
SHERIFF'S OFFICE
HERE, LUKE. MY LAST CIGAR – AS A TOKEN OF GRATITUDE.
OH, THANKS.
MR LUKE?
WHERE'RE YOU GOING, MR LUKE?
BUTCHER'S Shop
UNCLE HENRY SAYS YOU ALSO GOT THE DALTON COUSINS! IS IT TRUE? IS IT?
CAN WE COME WITH YOU?
IS IT TRUE YOU SHOT PHIL WIRE?
FLOK
FLOK
TELL US, MR LUKE!
PLEASE!
KILLING A MAN IS WRONG, KID ...
YOU TAKE FROM HIM EVERYTHING HE HAS ... AND EVERYTHING HE COULD HAVE HAD.
ENOUGH! SHOO! GO ON, GIT, KIDS! AND STOP BOTHERING MR LUKE!
AWWWW ...
17
HAHAHA! UNBELIEVABLE! YOU ARE QUITE THE STAR, LUCKY LUKE!
STILL ... BACK IN THE SHERIFF'S OFFICE, I THOUGHT YOU MIGHT ACTUALLY LOSE YOUR FAMOUS COOL.
IS IT THE LACK OF TOBACCO THAT'S GOT YOU SO HIGH-STRUNG?

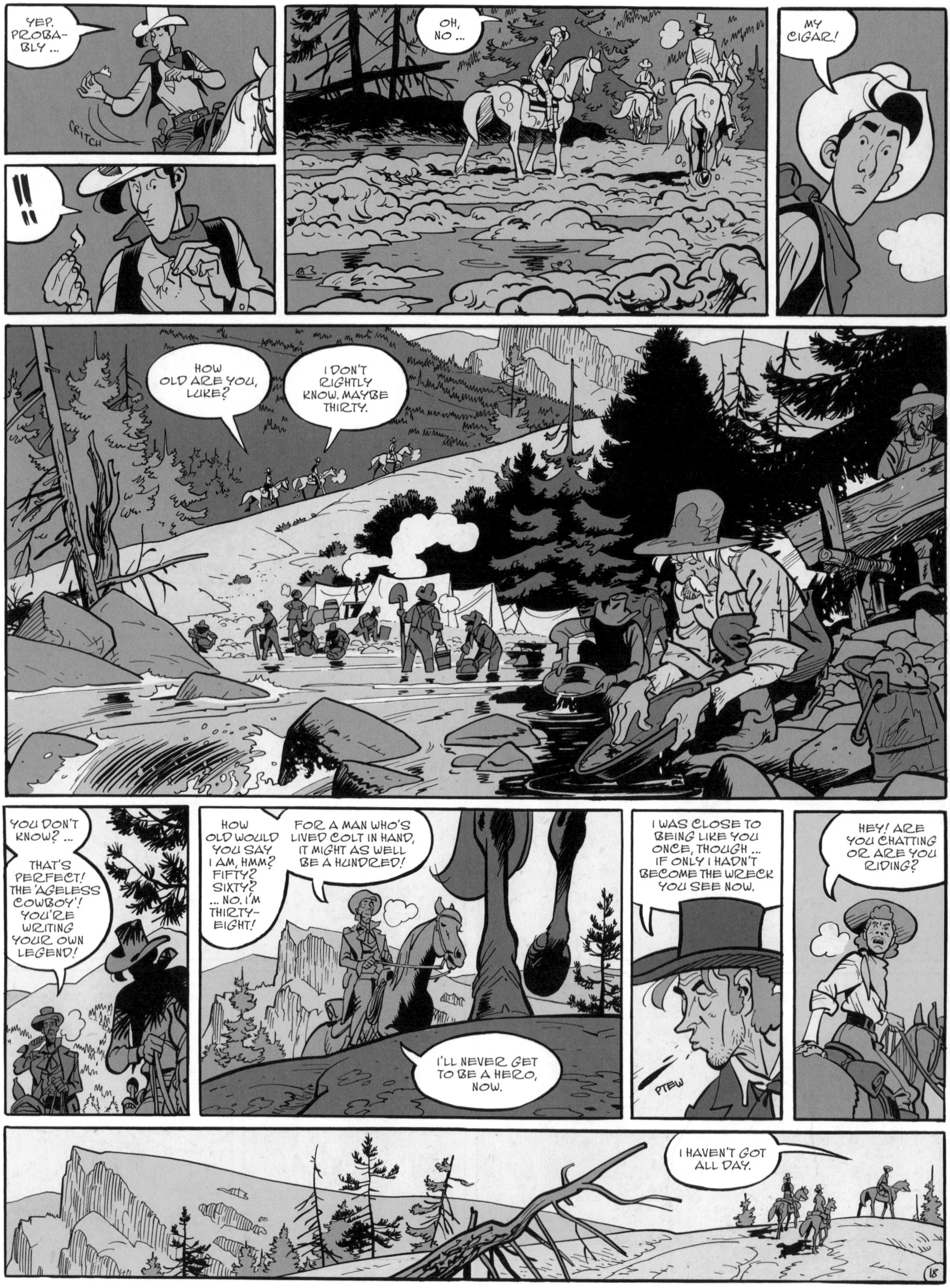
YEP. PROBA-BLY ...
CRITCH
!!
OH, NO ...
MY CIGAR!
HOW OLD ARE YOU, LUKE?
I DON'T RIGHTLY KNOW. MAYBE THIRTY.
YOU DON'T KNOW? ...
THAT'S PERFECT! THE 'AGELESS COWBOY'! YOU'RE WRITING YOUR OWN LEGEND!
HOW OLD WOULD YOU SAY I AM, HMM? FIFTY? SIXTY? ... NO, I'M THIRTY-EIGHT!
FOR A MAN WHO'S LIVED COLT IN HAND, IT MIGHT AS WELL BE A HUNDRED!
I'LL NEVER GET TO BE A HERO, NOW.
I WAS CLOSE TO BEING LIKE YOU ONCE, THOUGH ... IF ONLY I HADN'T BECOME THE WRECK YOU SEE NOW.
PTEW
HEY! ARE YOU CHATTING OR ARE YOU RIDING?
I HAVEN'T GOT ALL DAY.
18

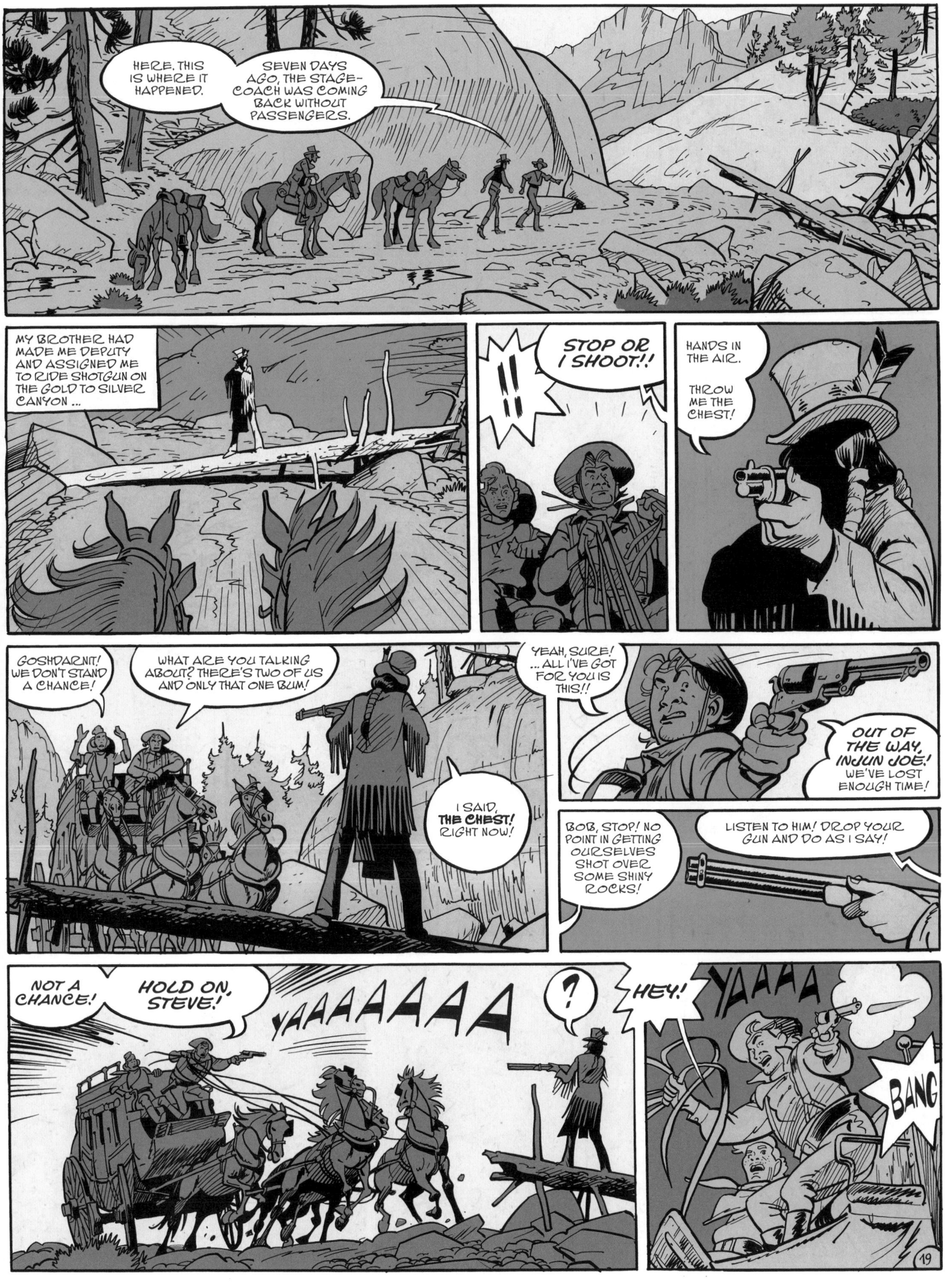
HERE. THIS IS WHERE IT HAPPENED.
SEVEN DAYS AGO, THE STAGE-COACH WAS COMING BACK WITHOUT PASSENGERS.
MY BROTHER HAD MADE ME DEPUTY AND ASSIGNED ME TO RIDE SHOTGUN ON THE GOLD TO SILVER CANYON ...
!!
STOP OR I SHOOT!!
HANDS IN THE AIR.
THROW ME THE CHEST!
GOSHDARNIT! WE DON'T STAND A CHANCE!
WHAT ARE YOU TALKING ABOUT? THERE'S TWO OF US AND ONLY THAT ONE BUM!
I SAID, THE CHEST! RIGHT NOW!
YEAH, SURE! ... ALL I'VE GOT FOR YOU IS THIS!!
OUT OF THE WAY, INJUN JOE! WE'VE LOST ENOUGH TIME!
BOB, STOP! NO POINT IN GETTING OURSELVES SHOT OVER SOME SHINY ROCKS!
LISTEN TO HIM! DROP YOUR GUN AND DO AS I SAY!
NOT A CHANCE!
HOLD ON, STEVE!
YAAAAAAA
?
HEY!
YAAAA
BANG
19

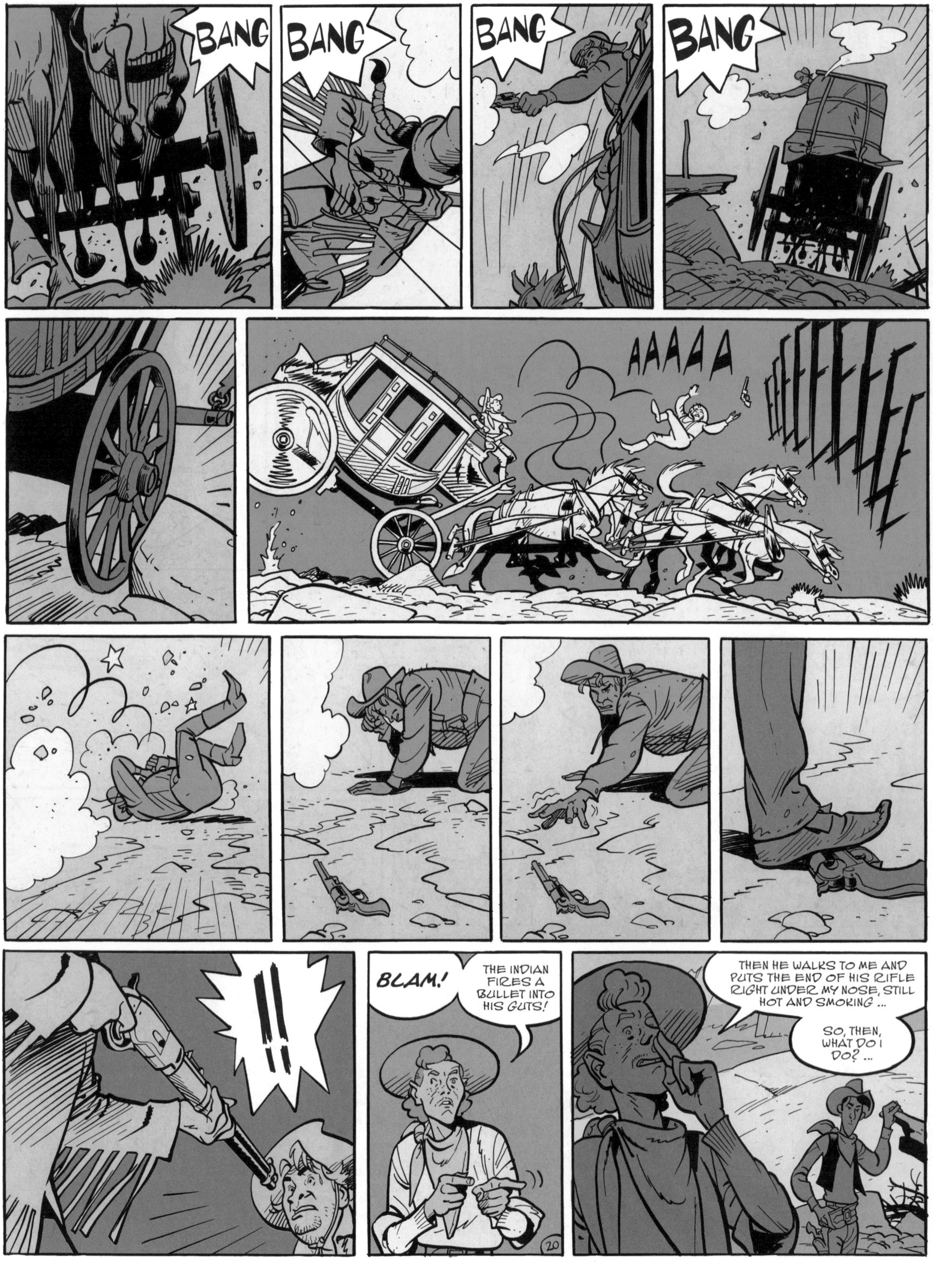
BANG
BANG
BANG
BANG
AAAAA
EEEEEEEE
!!
BLAM!
THE INDIAN FIRES A BULLET INTO HIS GUTS!
THEN HE WALKS TO ME AND PUTS THE END OF HIS RIFLE RIGHT UNDER MY NOSE, STILL HOT AND SMOKING ...
SO, THEN, WHAT DO I DO? ...
20

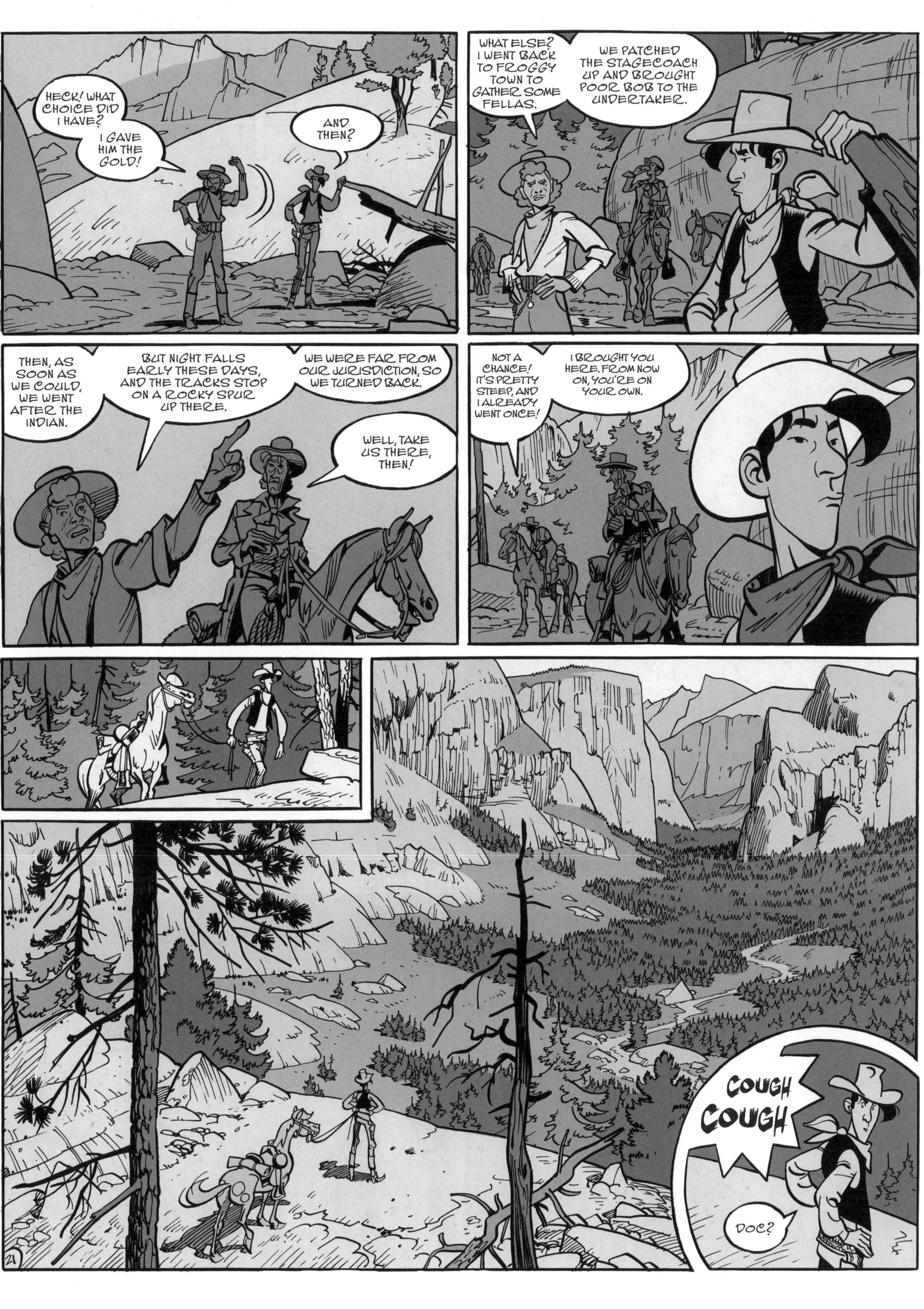
HECK! WHAT CHOICE DID I HAVE? I GAVE HIM THE GOLD!
AND THEN?
WHAT ELSE? I WENT BACK TO FROGGY TOWN TO GATHER SOME FELLAS.
WE PATCHED THE STAGECOACH UP AND BROUGHT POOR BOB TO THE UNDERTAKER.
THEN, AS SOON AS WE COULD, WE WENT AFTER THE INDIAN.
BUT NIGHT FALLS EARLY THESE DAYS, AND THE TRACKS STOP ON A ROCKY SPUR UP THERE.
WE WERE FAR FROM OUR JURISDICTION, SO WE TURNED BACK.
WELL, TAKE US THERE, THEN!
NOT A CHANCE! IT'S PRETTY STEEP, AND I ALREADY WENT ONCE!
I BROUGHT YOU HERE. FROM NOW ON, YOU'RE ON YOUR OWN.
COUGH COUGH
DOC?
21

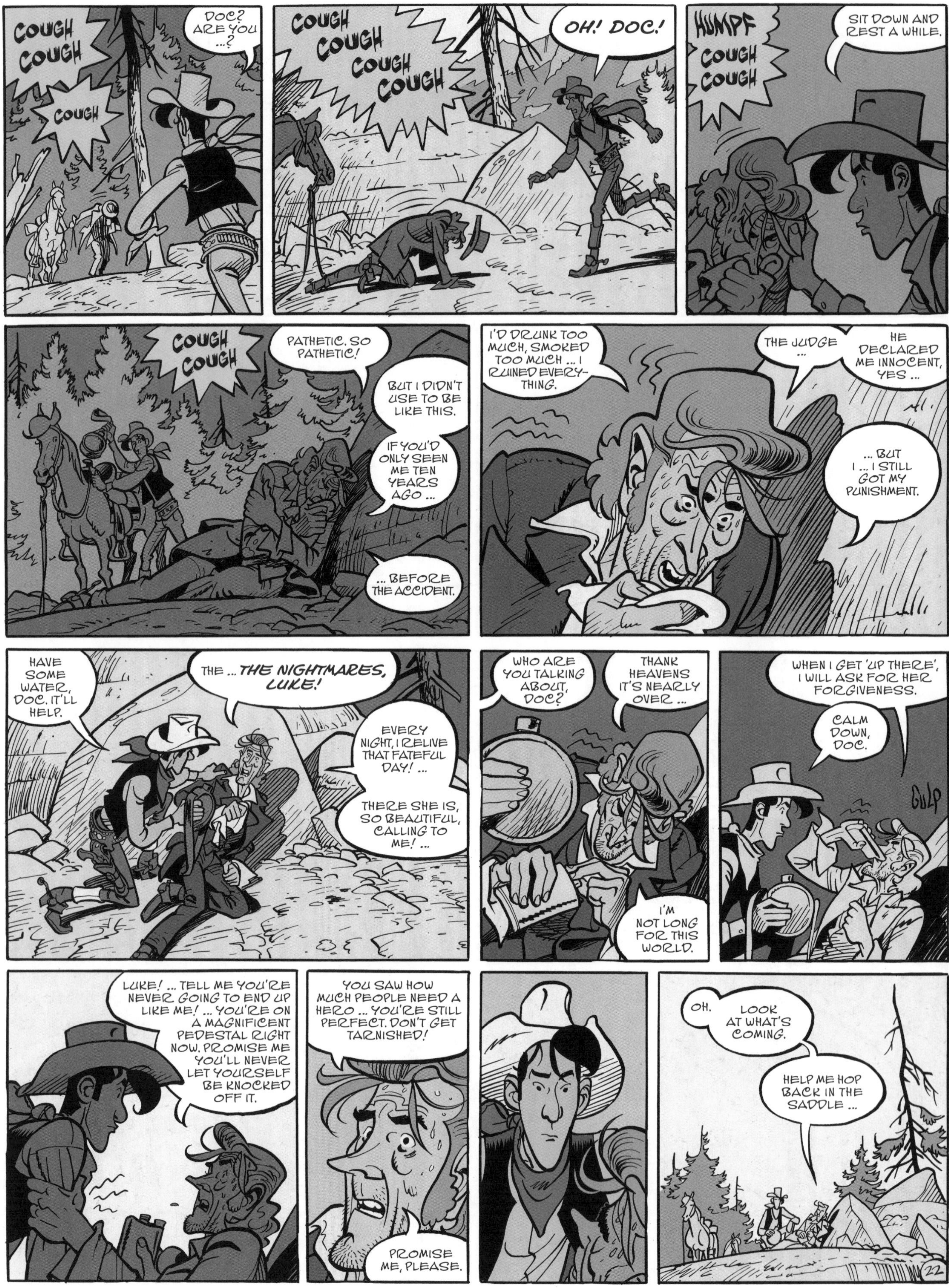
COUGH COUGH
COUGH
DOC? ARE YOU ...?
COUGH COUGH COUGH COUGH
OH! DOC!
HUMPF COUGH COUGH
SIT DOWN AND REST A WHILE.
COUGH COUGH
PATHETIC. SO PATHETIC!
BUT I DIDN'T USE TO BE LIKE THIS.
IF YOU'D ONLY SEEN ME TEN YEARS AGO ...
... BEFORE THE ACCIDENT.
I'D DRUNK TOO MUCH, SMOKED TOO MUCH ... I RUINED EVERY-THING.
THE JUDGE ...
HE DECLARED ME INNOCENT, YES ...
... BUT I ... I STILL GOT MY PUNISHMENT.
HAVE SOME WATER, DOC. IT'LL HELP.
THE ... THE NIGHTMARES, LUKE!
EVERY NIGHT, I RELIVE THAT FATEFUL DAY! ...
THERE SHE IS, SO BEAUTIFUL, CALLING TO ME! ...
WHO ARE YOU TALKING ABOUT, DOC?
THANK HEAVENS IT'S NEARLY OVER ...
I'M NOT LONG FOR THIS WORLD.
WHEN I GET 'UP THERE', I WILL ASK FOR HER FORGIVENESS.
CALM DOWN, DOC.
GULP
LUKE! ... TELL ME YOU'RE NEVER GOING TO END UP LIKE ME! ... YOU'RE ON A MAGNIFICENT PEDESTAL RIGHT NOW. PROMISE ME YOU'LL NEVER LET YOURSELF BE KNOCKED OFF IT.
YOU SAW HOW MUCH PEOPLE NEED A HERO ... YOU'RE STILL PERFECT. DON'T GET TARNISHED!
PROMISE ME, PLEASE.
OH.
LOOK AT WHAT'S COMING.
HELP ME HOP BACK IN THE SADDLE ...
22

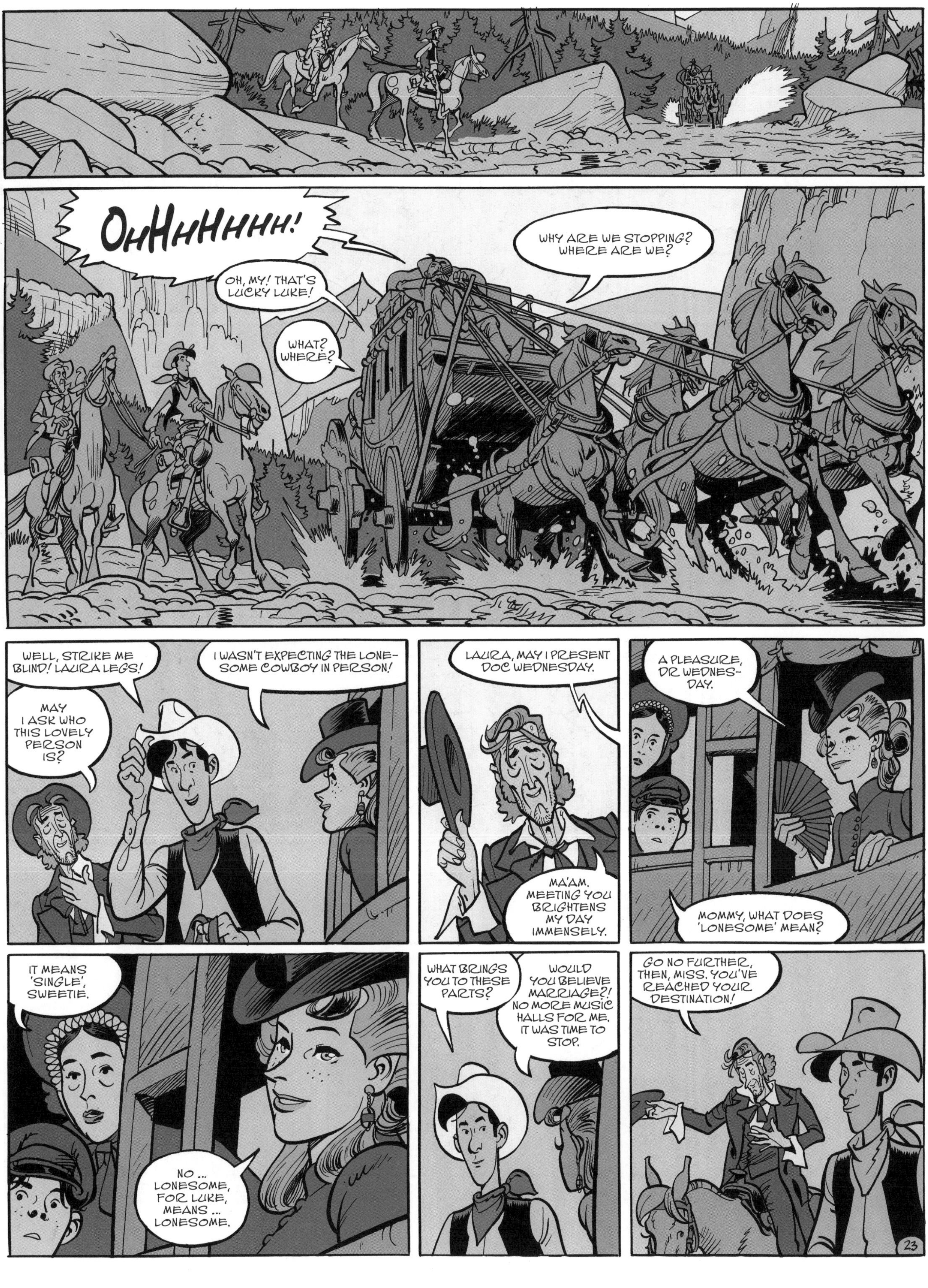
OhHhHhhh!
OH, MY! THAT'S LUCKY LUKE!
WHY ARE WE STOPPING? WHERE ARE WE?
WHAT? WHERE?
WELL, STRIKE ME BLIND! LAURA LEGS!
I WASN'T EXPECTING THE LONESOME COWBOY IN PERSON!
MAY I ASK WHO THIS LOVELY PERSON IS?
LAURA, MAY I PRESENT DOC WEDNESDAY.
MA'AM. MEETING YOU BRIGHTENS MY DAY IMMENSELY.
A PLEASURE, DR WEDNESDAY.
MOMMY, WHAT DOES 'LONESOME' MEAN?
IT MEANS 'SINGLE', SWEETIE.
NO ... LONESOME, FOR LUKE, MEANS ... LONESOME.
WHAT BRINGS YOU TO THESE PARTS?
WOULD YOU BELIEVE MARRIAGE?! NO MORE MUSIC HALLS FOR ME. IT WAS TIME TO STOP.
GO NO FURTHER, THEN, MISS. YOU'VE REACHED YOUR DESTINATION!
23

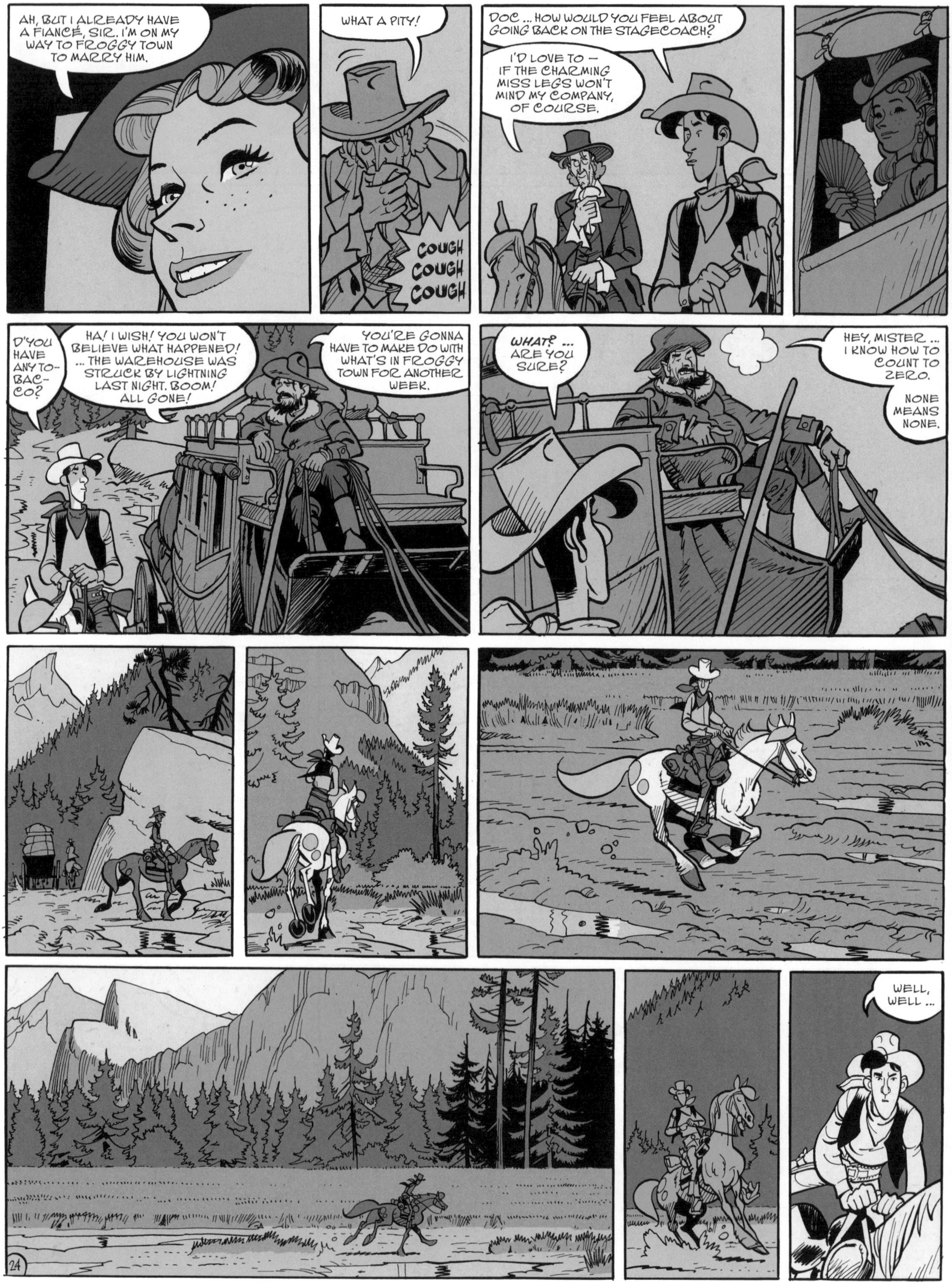

AH, BUT I ALREADY HAVE A FIANCÉ, SIR. I'M ON MY WAY TO FROGGY TOWN TO MARRY HIM.
WHAT A PITY!
COUGH COUGH COUGH
DOC ... HOW WOULD YOU FEEL ABOUT GOING BACK ON THE STAGECOACH?
I'D LOVE TO — IF THE CHARMING MISS LEGS WON'T MIND MY COMPANY, OF COURSE.
D'YOU HAVE ANY TO-BAC-CO?
HA! I WISH! YOU WON'T BELIEVE WHAT HAPPENED! ... THE WAREHOUSE WAS STRUCK BY LIGHTNING LAST NIGHT. BOOM! ALL GONE!
YOU'RE GONNA HAVE TO MAKE DO WITH WHAT'S IN FROGGY TOWN FOR ANOTHER WEEK.
WHAT? ... ARE YOU SURE?
HEY, MISTER ... I KNOW HOW TO COUNT TO ZERO.
NONE MEANS NONE.
WELL, WELL ...
24

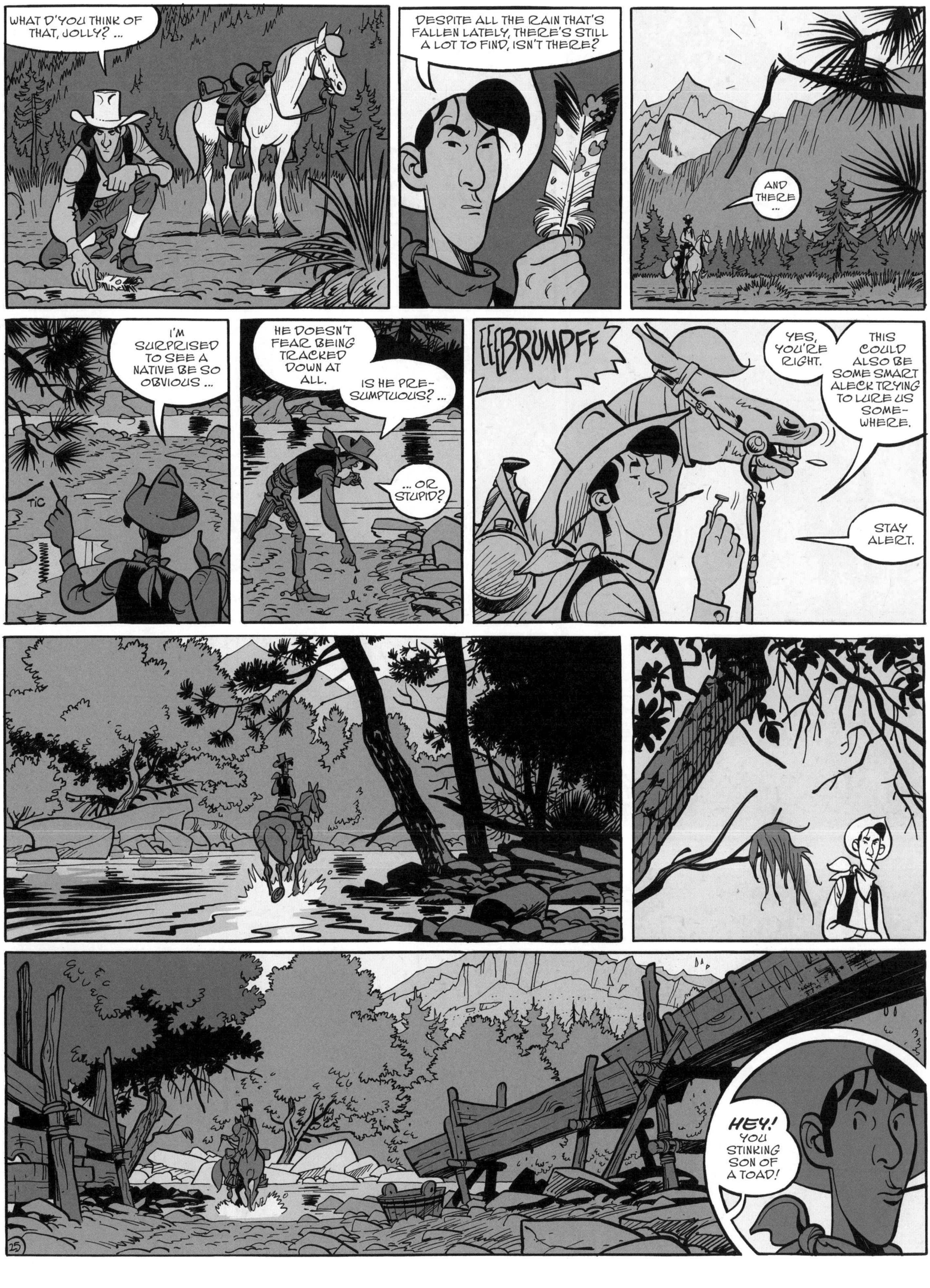
WHAT D'YOU THINK OF THAT, JOLLY? ...
DESPITE ALL THE RAIN THAT'S FALLEN LATELY, THERE'S STILL A LOT TO FIND, ISN'T THERE?
AND THERE ...
I'M SURPRISED TO SEE A NATIVE BE SO OBVIOUS ...
TIC
HE DOESN'T FEAR BEING TRACKED DOWN AT ALL.
IS HE PRE-SUMPTUOUS? ...
... OR STUPID?
EEEBRUMPFF
YES, YOU'RE RIGHT.
THIS COULD ALSO BE SOME SMART ALECK TRYING TO LURE US SOME-WHERE.
STAY ALERT.
HEY! YOU STINKING SON OF A TOAD!
25

THIS IS MY PROPERTY! GET OFF MY LAND RIGHT NOW!

OH ... I DIDN'T SEE ANYONE, SO I TOOK THE LIBERTY OF—

DOES IT LOOK TO YOU LIKE I CARE? STUFF YOUR LIBERTY! GIT!

I'M LOOKING FOR THE NATIVE WHO ROBBED THE STAGECOACH.

HIS TRACKS LEAD THIS WAY. YOU HAVEN'T SEEN HIM ...?

HIS HORSE MUST HAVE BEEN LIMPING SLIGHTLY. ONE OF HIS SHOES LOST A NAIL.

IF I'D SEEN ONE OF THEM, HE'D BE AS STIFF AS MY CRUTCH RIGHT NOW! I SHOOT INJUNS ON SIGHT ... SO DON'T COME NOSING AROUND HERE AND TRY TO PIN WHO-KNOWS-WHAT MISCHIEF ON ME!

I DON'T KNOW YOU, MISTER, BUT I CAN TELL A SNAKE NO MATTER WHAT HOLE HE CRAWLED OUT OF!

PTEW!

PLOTSH

?

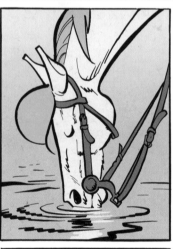

HEY!

FFFFF

AARH! ... GIT ON OUTTA HERE, YOU AND THAT NAG!!

CLICK

26

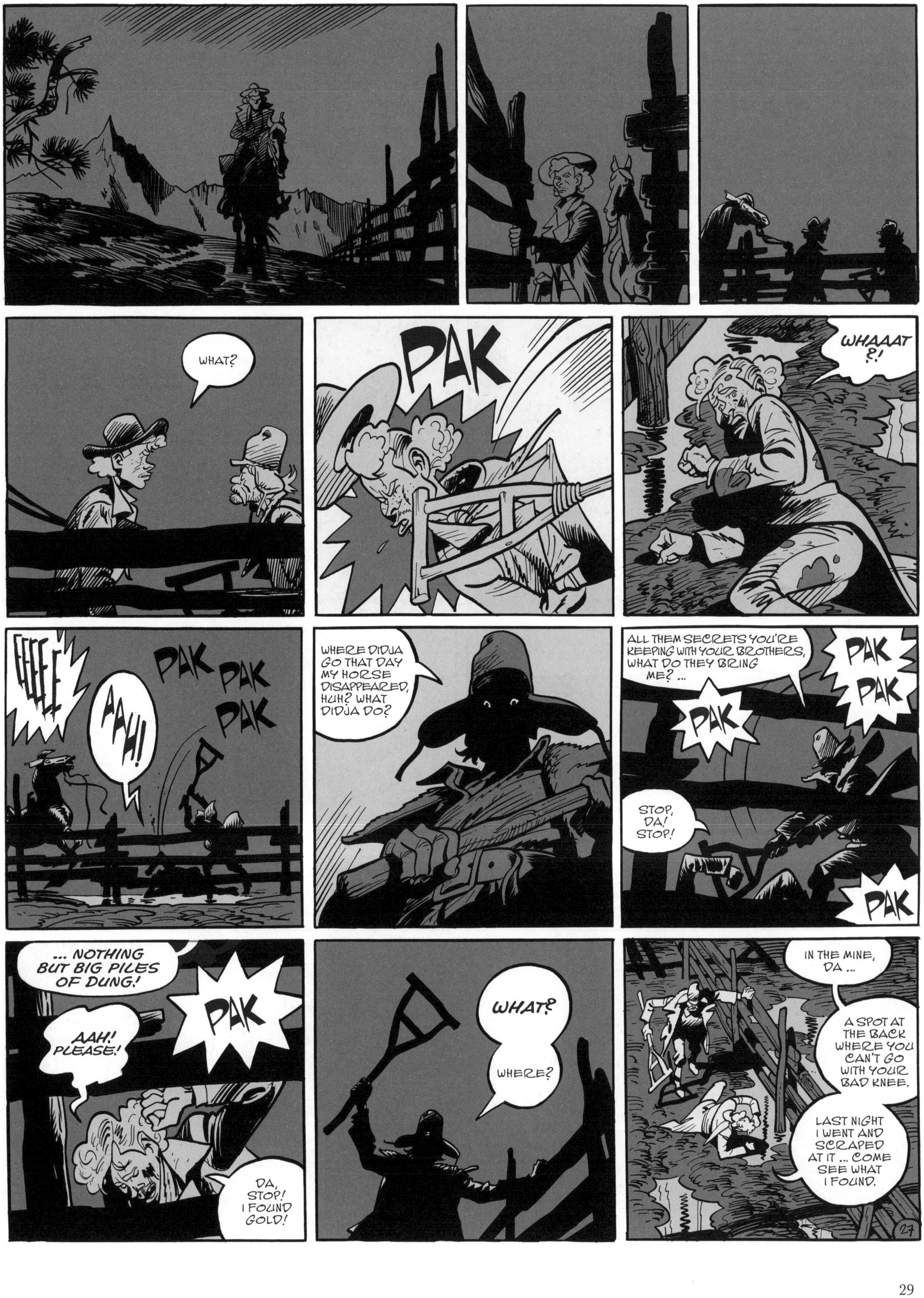
WHAT?
PAK
WHAAAT ?!
EEEEE
PAK PAK PAK
AAH!
WHERE DIDJA GO THAT DAY MY HORSE DISAPPEARED, HUH? WHAT DIDJA DO?
ALL THEM SECRETS YOU'RE KEEPING WITH YOUR BROTHERS, WHAT DO THEY BRING ME? ...
PAK PAK
PAK
STOP, DA! STOP!
PAK
... NOTHING BUT BIG PILES OF DUNG!
PAK
AAH! PLEASE!
DA, STOP! I FOUND GOLD!
WHAT?
WHERE?
IN THE MINE, DA ...
A SPOT AT THE BACK WHERE YOU CAN'T GO WITH YOUR BAD KNEE.
LAST NIGHT I WENT AND SCRAPED AT IT ... COME SEE WHAT I FOUND.
27

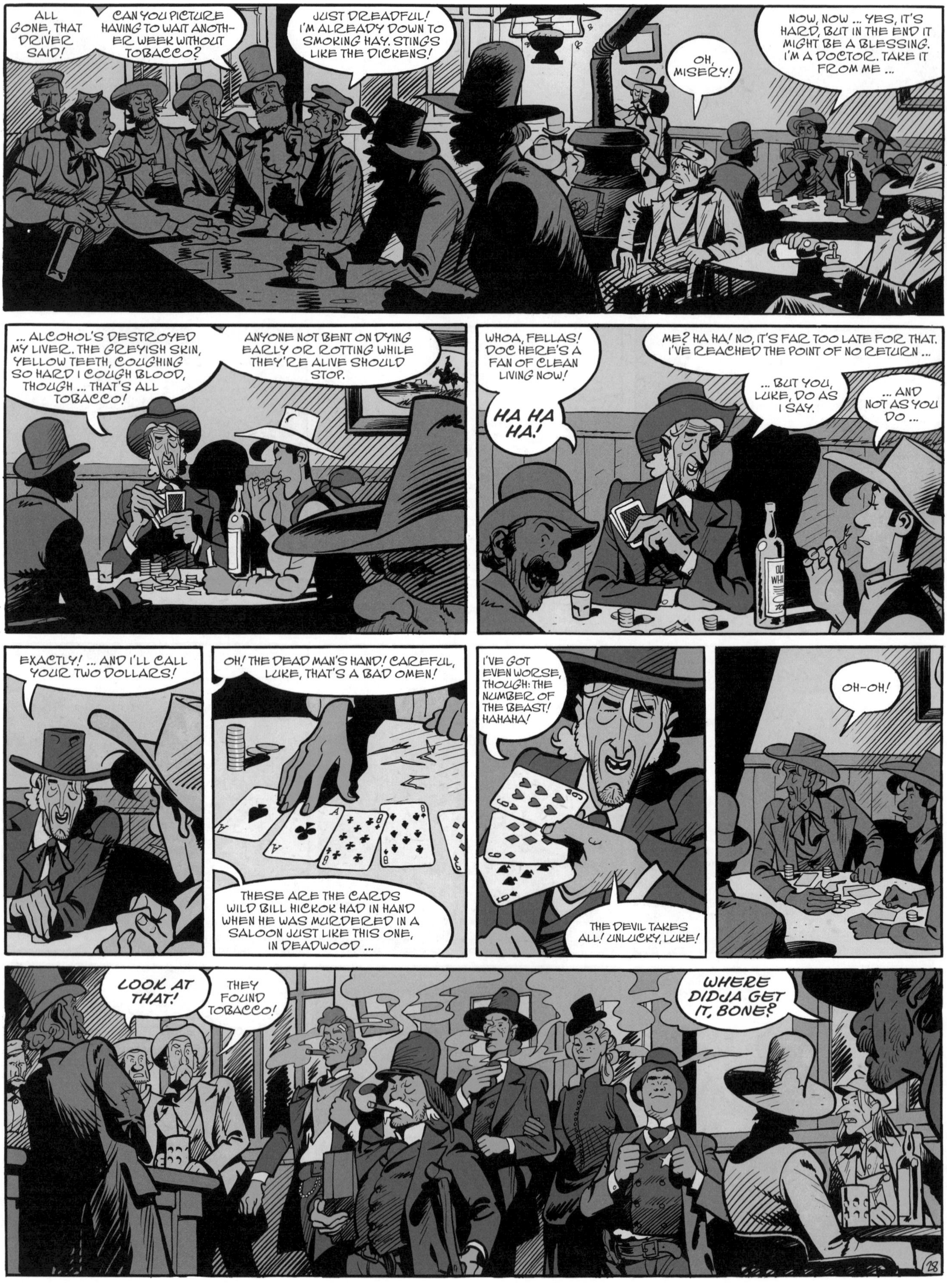
ALL GONE, THAT DRIVER SAID!
CAN YOU PICTURE HAVING TO WAIT ANOTHER WEEK WITHOUT TOBACCO?
JUST DREADFUL! I'M ALREADY DOWN TO SMOKING HAY. STINGS LIKE THE DICKENS!
OH, MISERY!
NOW, NOW ... YES, IT'S HARD, BUT IN THE END IT MIGHT BE A BLESSING. I'M A DOCTOR. TAKE IT FROM ME ...
... ALCOHOL'S DESTROYED MY LIVER. THE GREYISH SKIN, YELLOW TEETH, COUGHING SO HARD I COUGH BLOOD, THOUGH ... THAT'S ALL TOBACCO!
ANYONE NOT BENT ON DYING EARLY OR ROTTING WHILE THEY'RE ALIVE SHOULD STOP.
WHOA, FELLAS! DOC HERE'S A FAN OF CLEAN LIVING NOW!
HA HA HA!
ME? HA HA! NO, IT'S FAR TOO LATE FOR THAT. I'VE REACHED THE POINT OF NO RETURN ...
... BUT YOU, LUKE, DO AS I SAY.
... AND NOT AS YOU DO ...
EXACTLY! ... AND I'LL CALL YOUR TWO DOLLARS!
OH! THE DEAD MAN'S HAND! CAREFUL, LUKE, THAT'S A BAD OMEN!
THESE ARE THE CARDS WILD BILL HICKOK HAD IN HAND WHEN HE WAS MURDERED IN A SALOON JUST LIKE THIS ONE, IN DEADWOOD ...
I'VE GOT EVEN WORSE, THOUGH: THE NUMBER OF THE BEAST! HAHAHA!
THE DEVIL TAKES ALL! UNLUCKY, LUKE!
OH-OH!
LOOK AT THAT!
THEY FOUND TOBACCO!
WHERE DIDJA GET IT, BONE?
28

FROM THAT OLD CROOK SMITH! ALL THAT WAS LEFT OF HIS PERSONAL STASH. SOLD IT TO ME FOR ITS WEIGHT ...

... IN GOLD!

PAK

MY LUCK'S TURNED, FELLAS! MY MINE'S DECIDED TO SPIT OUT A FEW MORE ROCKS FOR OLD BONE!

THIS ROUND'S ON ME! WHO WANTS A CIGAR?

WOO, THANKS!

HERE.

HERE.

YOU TOO, TAKE ONE.

THANKS, BONE!

AND YOU TOO, OVER THERE.

OH, BUT NO, NOT YOU!

?!

CLAP

HUH? WHY NOT, BONE?

BECAUSE THIS ONE HERE'S NOTHING BUT A SLIMY TOAD. A DUNG STIRRER.

D'YOU KNOW WHAT HE DID TODAY, HUH? ... HE DONE RODE UP TO **MY HOME!** ... AND TO DO WHAT? ... TO SPIT ON THE BONES'S REPUTATION, THAT'S WHAT! FOR NO REASON, TOO! ... **NONE!**

NOT TRUE! I FOLLOWED TRACKS. SOMETHING THE SHERIFF AND YOUR OTHER SONS HADN'T DONE BEFORE ...

WHICH IS STRANGE, BECAUSE IT WAS A CLEAR TRAIL EVEN AFTER A WEEK OF RAIN!

I FOUND THIS, WHICH LED ME TO YOUR PLACE.

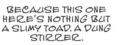

SO WHAT? YOU FIND A NAIL AND THAT'S ENOUGH TO COME INSULT US PUBLICLY?

YOU'VE ACCUSED US OF NOT DOING OUR JOB PROPERLY TOO MANY TIMES ALREADY.

ONE MORE REMARK LIKE THAT, AND ...

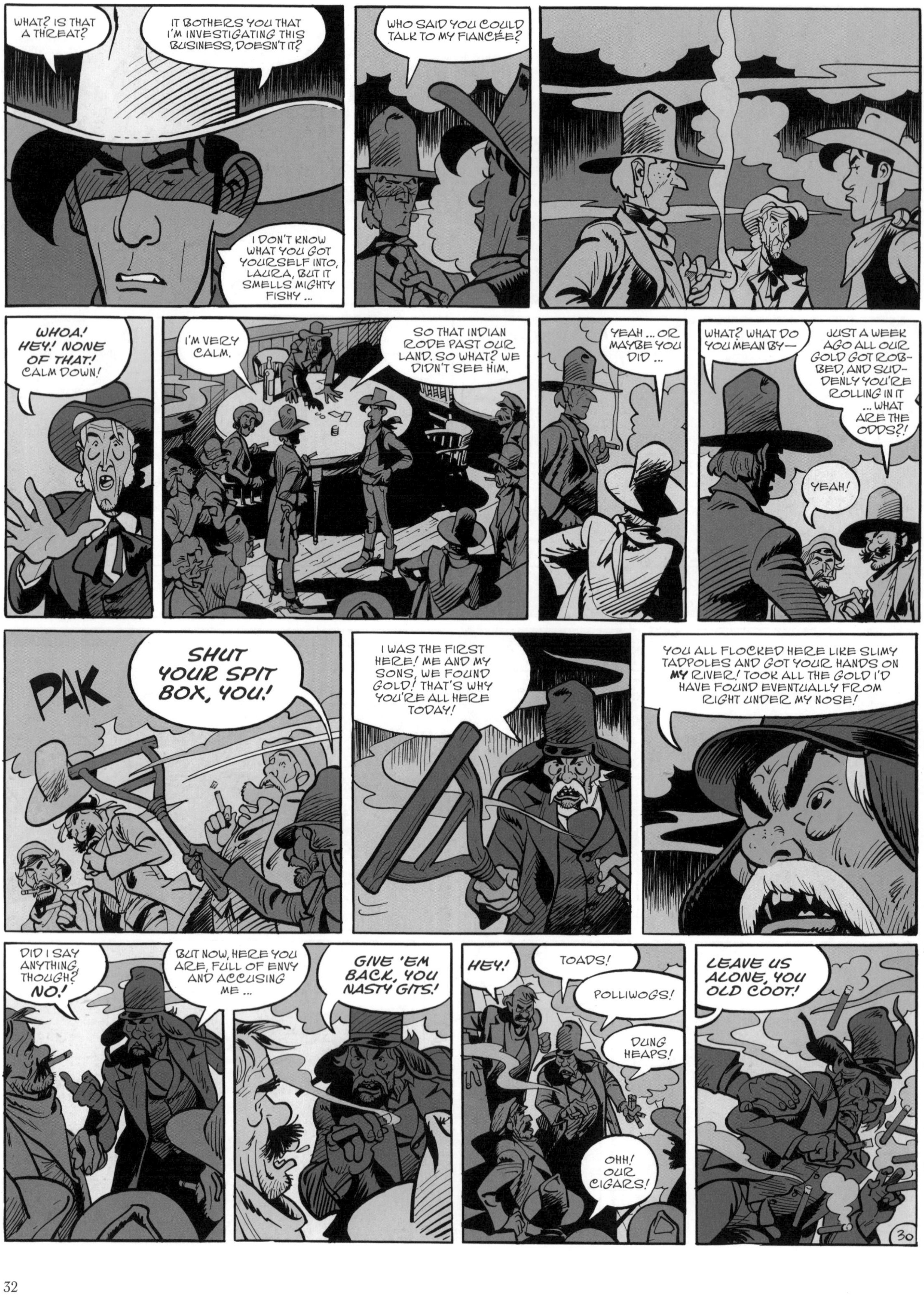
WHAT? IS THAT A THREAT?
IT BOTHERS YOU THAT I'M INVESTIGATING THIS BUSINESS, DOESN'T IT?
I DON'T KNOW WHAT YOU GOT YOURSELF INTO, LAURA, BUT IT SMELLS MIGHTY FISHY ...
WHO SAID YOU COULD TALK TO MY FIANCÉE?
WHOA! HEY! NONE OF THAT! CALM DOWN!
I'M VERY CALM.
SO THAT INDIAN RODE PAST OUR LAND. SO WHAT? WE DIDN'T SEE HIM.
YEAH ... OR MAYBE YOU DID ...
WHAT? WHAT DO YOU MEAN BY—
JUST A WEEK AGO ALL OUR GOLD GOT ROBBED, AND SUDDENLY YOU'RE ROLLING IN IT ... WHAT ARE THE ODDS?!
YEAH!
PAK
SHUT YOUR SPIT BOX, YOU!
I WAS THE FIRST HERE! ME AND MY SONS, WE FOUND GOLD! THAT'S WHY YOU'RE ALL HERE TODAY!
YOU ALL FLOCKED HERE LIKE SLIMY TADPOLES AND GOT YOUR HANDS ON MY RIVER! TOOK ALL THE GOLD I'D HAVE FOUND EVENTUALLY FROM RIGHT UNDER MY NOSE!
DID I SAY ANYTHING, THOUGH? NO!
BUT NOW, HERE YOU ARE, FULL OF ENVY AND ACCUSING ME ...
GIVE 'EM BACK, YOU NASTY GITS!
HEY!
TOADS!
POLLIWOGS!
DUNG HEAPS!
OHH! OUR CIGARS!
LEAVE US ALONE, YOU OLD COOT!
30

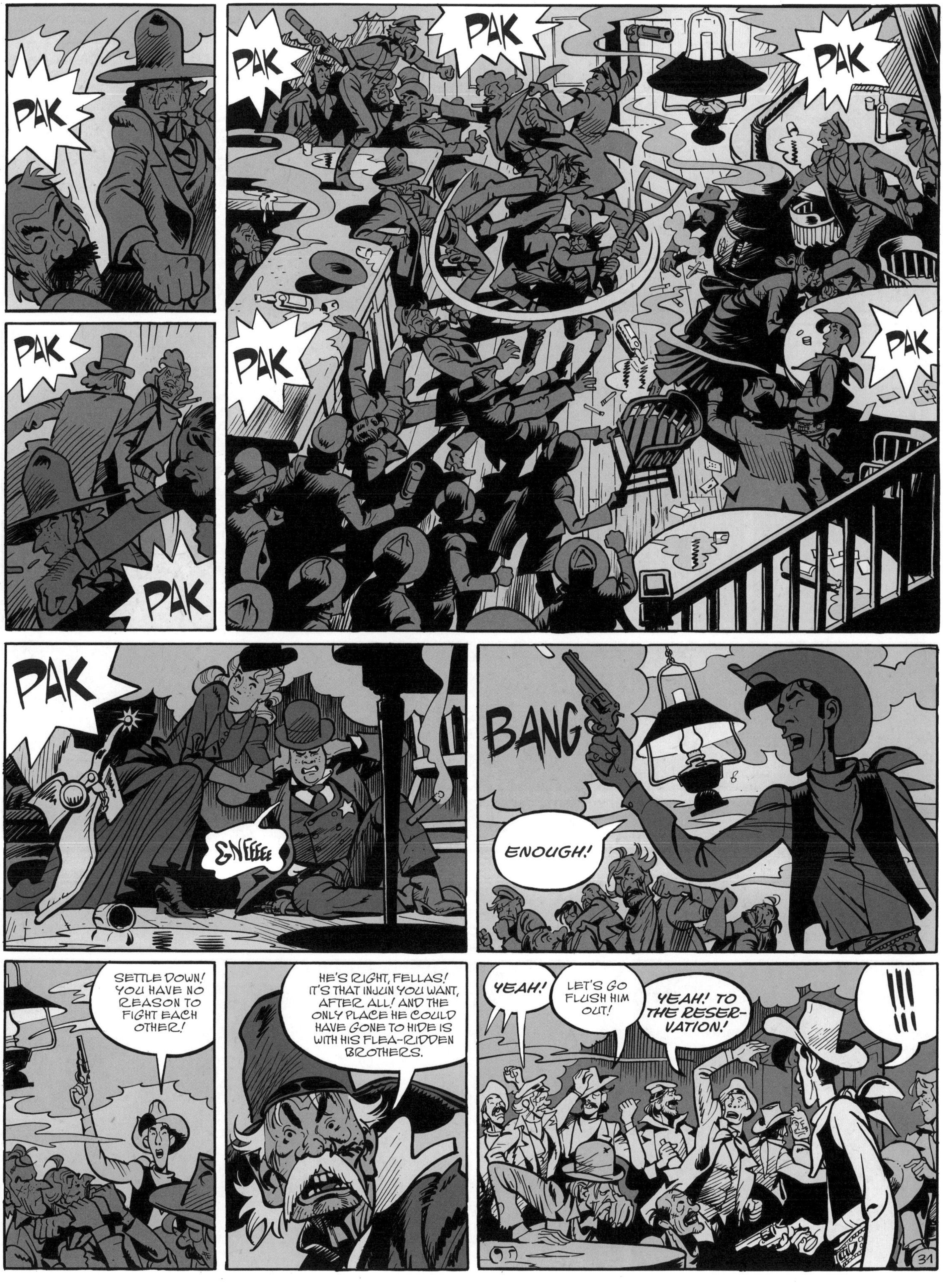

PAK
PAK
PAK
PAK
PAK
PAK
PAK
PAK
PAK
PAK
GNEEEEE
BANG
ENOUGH!
SETTLE DOWN! YOU HAVE NO REASON TO FIGHT EACH OTHER!
HE'S RIGHT, FELLAS! IT'S THAT INJUN YOU WANT, AFTER ALL! AND THE ONLY PLACE HE COULD HAVE GONE TO HIDE IS WITH HIS FLEA-RIDDEN BROTHERS.
YEAH!
LET'S GO FLUSH HIM OUT!
YEAH! TO THE RESER-VATION!
!!!
31

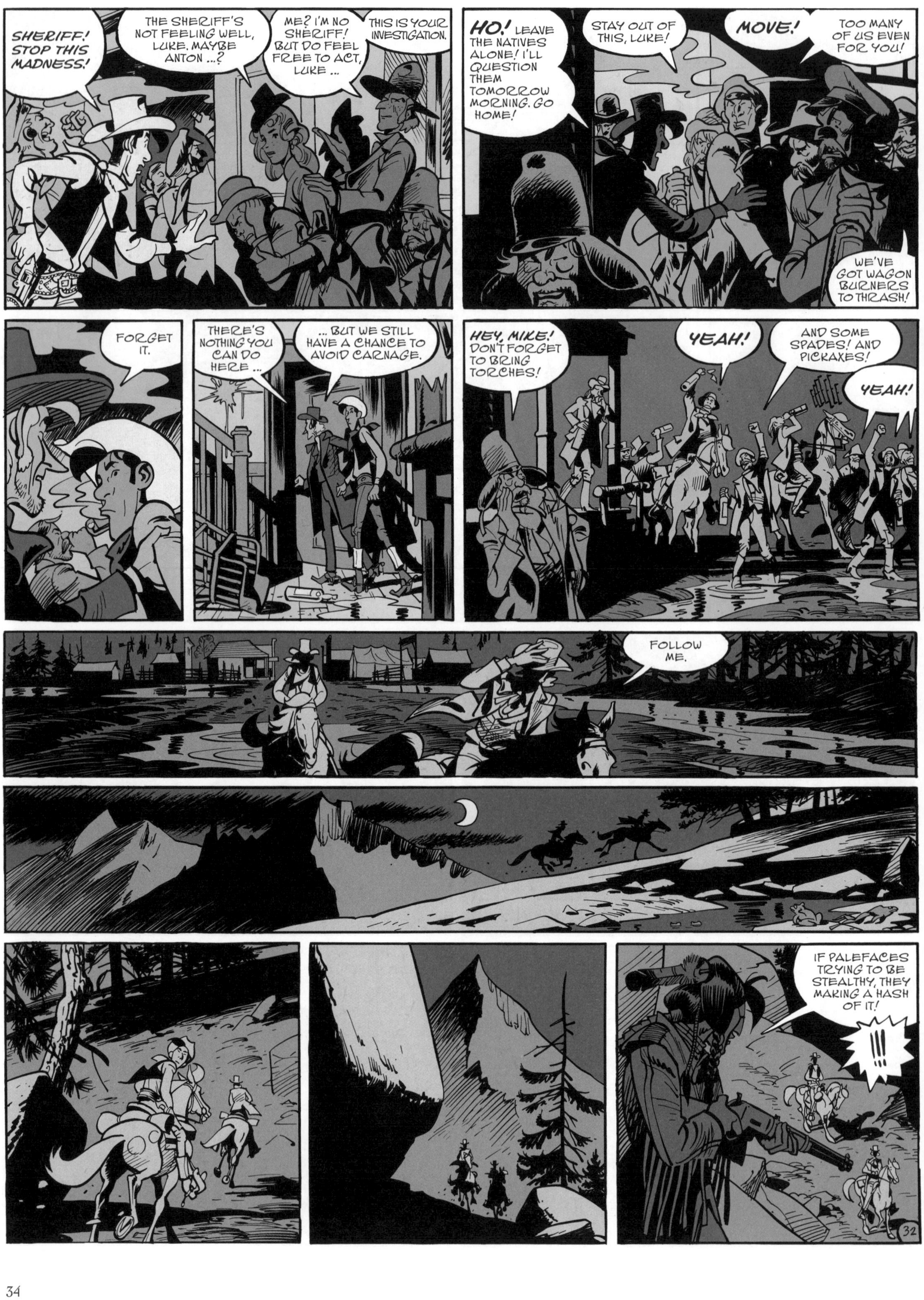

SHERIFF! STOP THIS MADNESS!
THE SHERIFF'S NOT FEELING WELL, LUKE. MAYBE ANTON ...?
ME? I'M NO SHERIFF! BUT DO FEEL FREE TO ACT, LUKE ...
THIS IS YOUR INVESTIGATION.
HO! LEAVE THE NATIVES ALONE! I'LL QUESTION THEM TOMORROW MORNING. GO HOME!
STAY OUT OF THIS, LUKE!
MOVE!
TOO MANY OF US EVEN FOR YOU!
WE'VE GOT WAGON BURNERS TO THRASH!
FORGET IT.
THERE'S NOTHING YOU CAN DO HERE ...
... BUT WE STILL HAVE A CHANCE TO AVOID CARNAGE.
HEY, MIKE! DON'T FORGET TO BRING TORCHES!
YEAH!
AND SOME SPADES! AND PICKAXES!
YEAH!
FOLLOW ME.
IF PALEFACES TRYING TO BE STEALTHY, THEY MAKING A HASH OF IT!
!!!
32

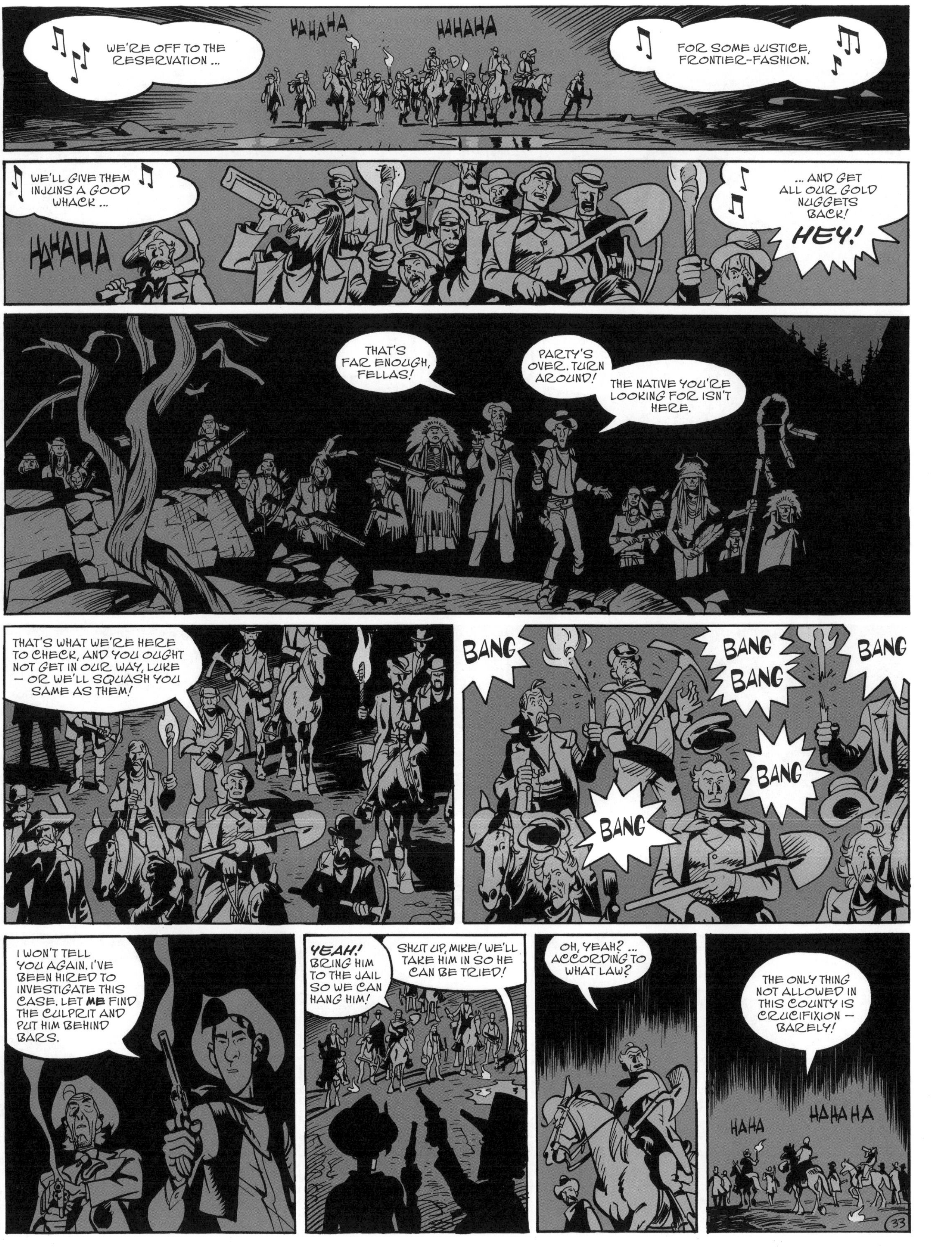

HAHAHA
HAHAHA
WE'RE OFF TO THE RESERVATION ...
FOR SOME JUSTICE, FRONTIER-FASHION.
WE'LL GIVE THEM INJUNS A GOOD WHACK ...
HAHAHA
... AND GET ALL OUR GOLD NUGGETS BACK!
HEY!
THAT'S FAR ENOUGH, FELLAS!
PARTY'S OVER. TURN AROUND!
THE NATIVE YOU'RE LOOKING FOR ISN'T HERE.
THAT'S WHAT WE'RE HERE TO CHECK, AND YOU OUGHT NOT GET IN OUR WAY, LUKE – OR WE'LL SQUASH YOU SAME AS THEM!
BANG
BANG
BANG
BANG
BANG
BANG
I WON'T TELL YOU AGAIN. I'VE BEEN HIRED TO INVESTIGATE THIS CASE. LET ME FIND THE CULPRIT AND PUT HIM BEHIND BARS.
YEAH! BRING HIM TO THE JAIL SO WE CAN HANG HIM!
SHUT UP, MIKE! WE'LL TAKE HIM IN SO HE CAN BE TRIED!
OH, YEAH? ... ACCORDING TO WHAT LAW?
THE ONLY THING NOT ALLOWED IN THIS COUNTY IS CRUCIFIXION – BARELY!
HAHA
HAHAHA
33

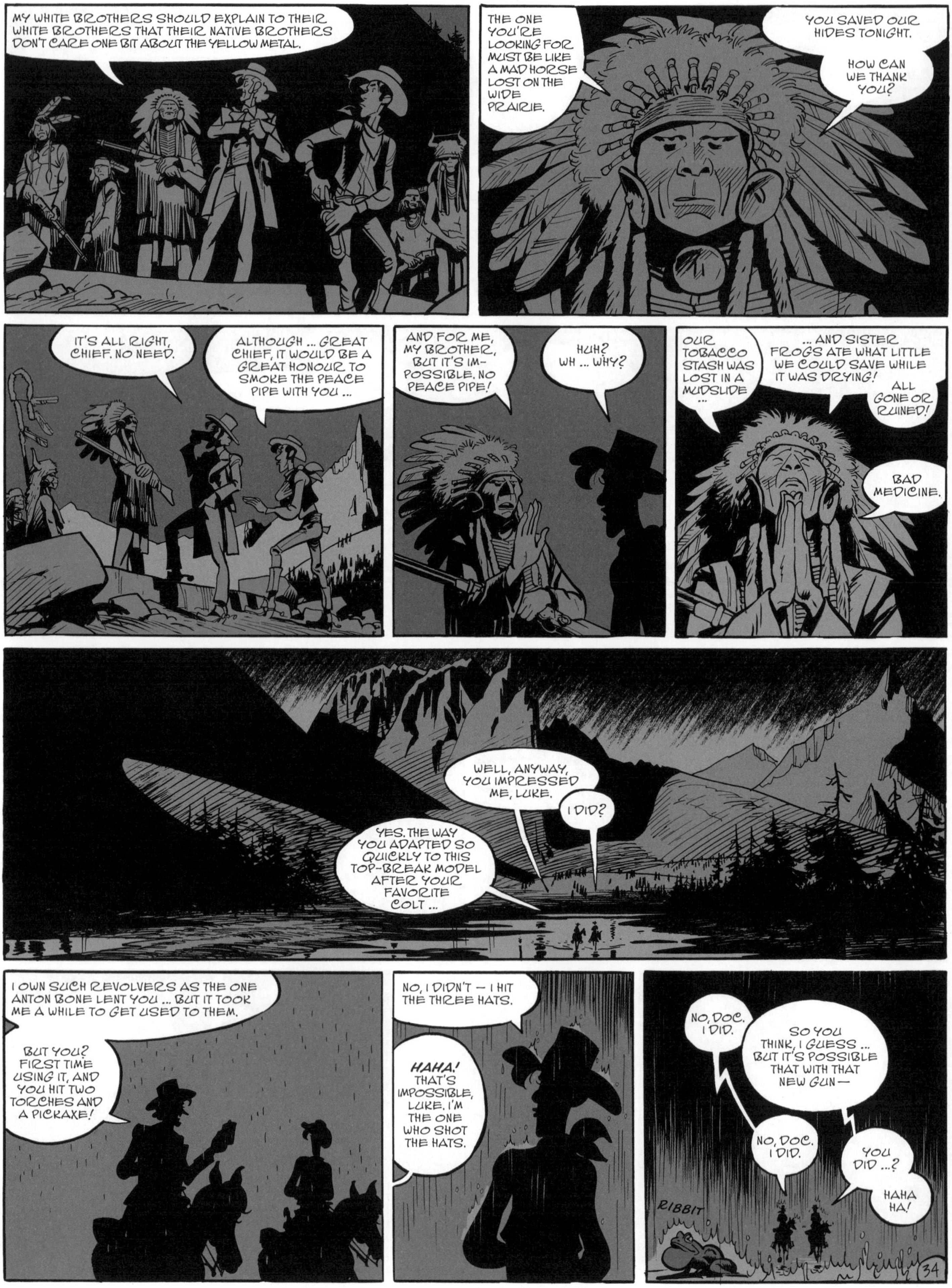
MY WHITE BROTHERS SHOULD EXPLAIN TO THEIR WHITE BROTHERS THAT THEIR NATIVE BROTHERS DON'T CARE ONE BIT ABOUT THE YELLOW METAL.
THE ONE YOU'RE LOOKING FOR MUST BE LIKE A MAD HORSE LOST ON THE WIDE PRAIRIE.
YOU SAVED OUR HIDES TONIGHT.
HOW CAN WE THANK YOU?
IT'S ALL RIGHT, CHIEF. NO NEED.
ALTHOUGH ... GREAT CHIEF, IT WOULD BE A GREAT HONOUR TO SMOKE THE PEACE PIPE WITH YOU ...
AND FOR ME, MY BROTHER, BUT IT'S IMPOSSIBLE. NO PEACE PIPE!
HUH? WH ... WHY?
OUR TOBACCO STASH WAS LOST IN A MUDSLIDE ...
... AND SISTER FROGS ATE WHAT LITTLE WE COULD SAVE WHILE IT WAS DRYING!
ALL GONE OR RUINED!
BAD MEDICINE.
WELL, ANYWAY, YOU IMPRESSED ME, LUKE.
I DID?
YES. THE WAY YOU ADAPTED SO QUICKLY TO THIS TOP-BREAK MODEL AFTER YOUR FAVORITE COLT ...
I OWN SUCH REVOLVERS AS THE ONE ANTON BONE LENT YOU ... BUT IT TOOK ME A WHILE TO GET USED TO THEM.
BUT YOU? FIRST TIME USING IT, AND YOU HIT TWO TORCHES AND A PICKAXE!
NO, I DIDN'T — I HIT THE THREE HATS.
HAHA! THAT'S IMPOSSIBLE, LUKE. I'M THE ONE WHO SHOT THE HATS.
NO, DOC. I DID.
SO YOU THINK, I GUESS ... BUT IT'S POSSIBLE THAT WITH THAT NEW GUN—
NO, DOC. I DID.
YOU DID ...?
HAHA HA!
RIBBIT
34

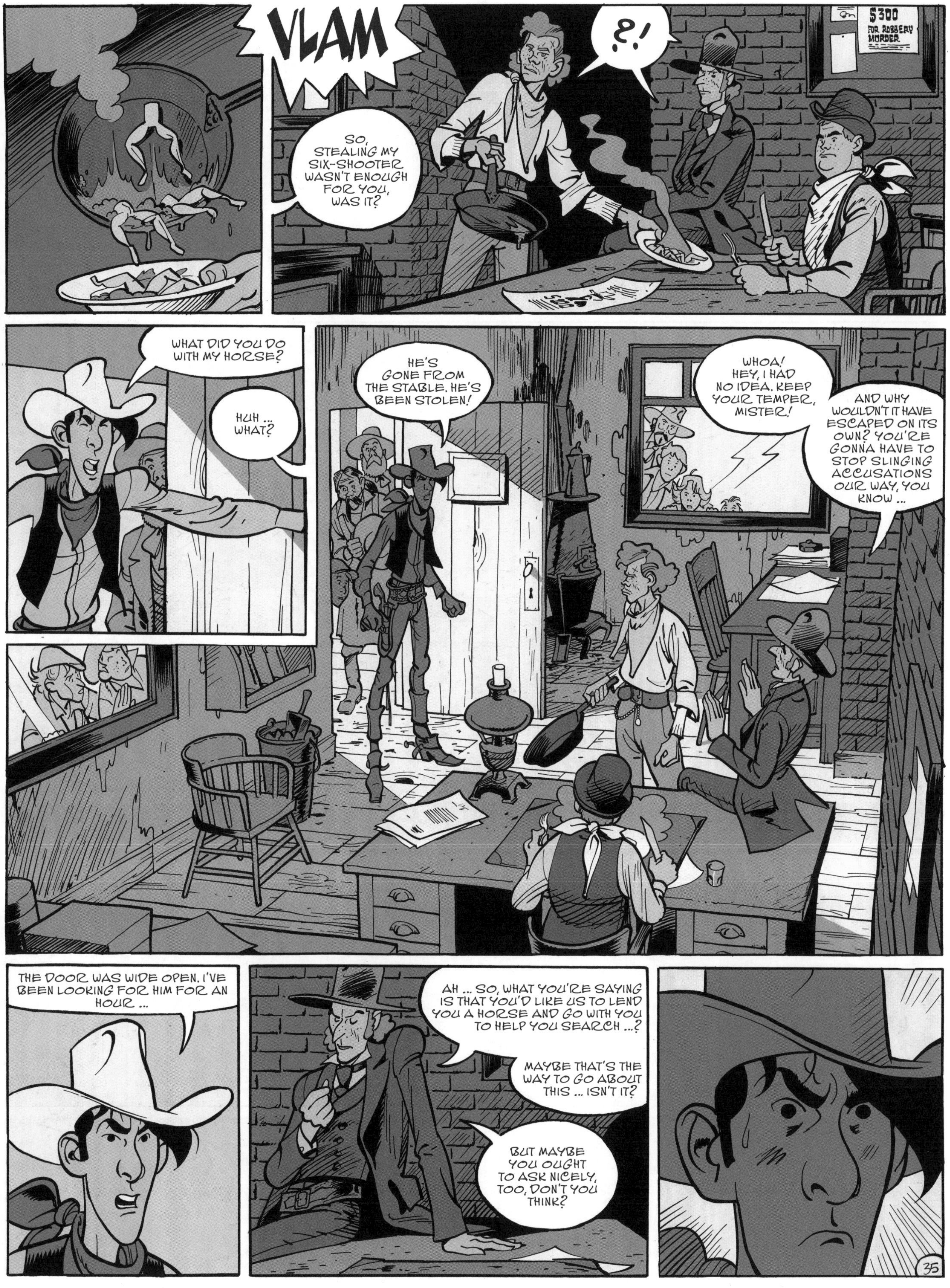
VLAM
?!
$300
FOR ROBBERY
MURDER
SO, STEALING MY SIX-SHOOTER WASN'T ENOUGH FOR YOU, WAS IT?
WHAT DID YOU DO WITH MY HORSE?
HUH ... WHAT?
HE'S GONE FROM THE STABLE. HE'S BEEN STOLEN!
WHOA! HEY, I HAD NO IDEA. KEEP YOUR TEMPER, MISTER!
AND WHY WOULDN'T IT HAVE ESCAPED ON ITS OWN? YOU'RE GONNA HAVE TO STOP SLINGING ACCUSATIONS OUR WAY, YOU KNOW ...
THE DOOR WAS WIDE OPEN. I'VE BEEN LOOKING FOR HIM FOR AN HOUR ...
AH ... SO, WHAT YOU'RE SAYING IS THAT YOU'D LIKE US TO LEND YOU A HORSE AND GO WITH YOU TO HELP YOU SEARCH ...?
MAYBE THAT'S THE WAY TO GO ABOUT THIS ... ISN'T IT?
BUT MAYBE YOU OUGHT TO ASK NICELY, TOO, DON'T YOU THINK?
35

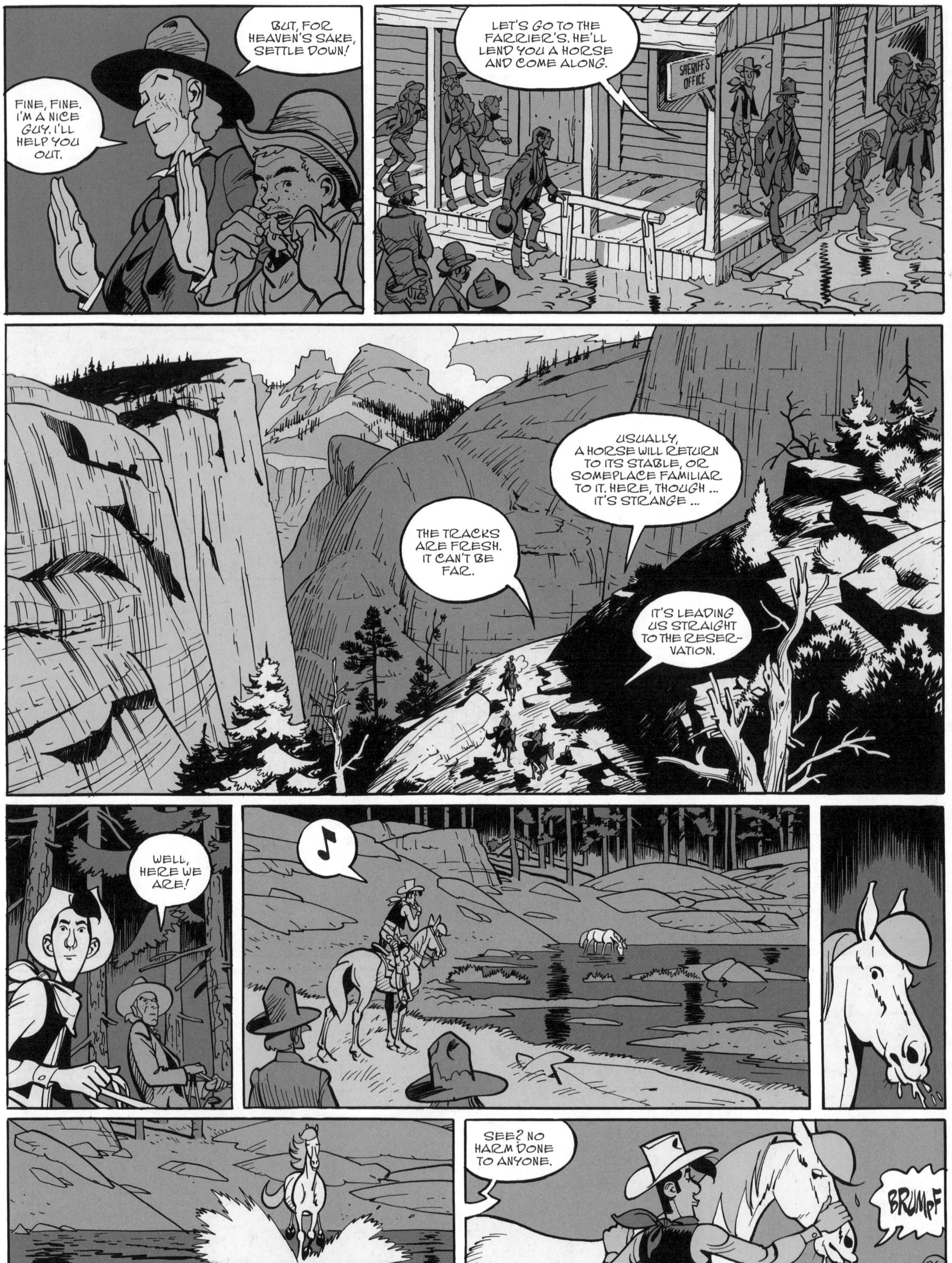
BUT, FOR HEAVEN'S SAKE, SETTLE DOWN!
FINE, FINE. I'M A NICE GUY. I'LL HELP YOU OUT.
LET'S GO TO THE FARRIER'S. HE'LL LEND YOU A HORSE AND COME ALONG.
SHERIFF'S OFFICE
USUALLY, A HORSE WILL RETURN TO ITS STABLE, OR SOMEPLACE FAMILIAR TO IT. HERE, THOUGH ... IT'S STRANGE ...
THE TRACKS ARE FRESH. IT CAN'T BE FAR.
IT'S LEADING US STRAIGHT TO THE RESER-VATION.
WELL, HERE WE ARE!
♪
SEE? NO HARM DONE TO ANYONE.
BRUMPF
36

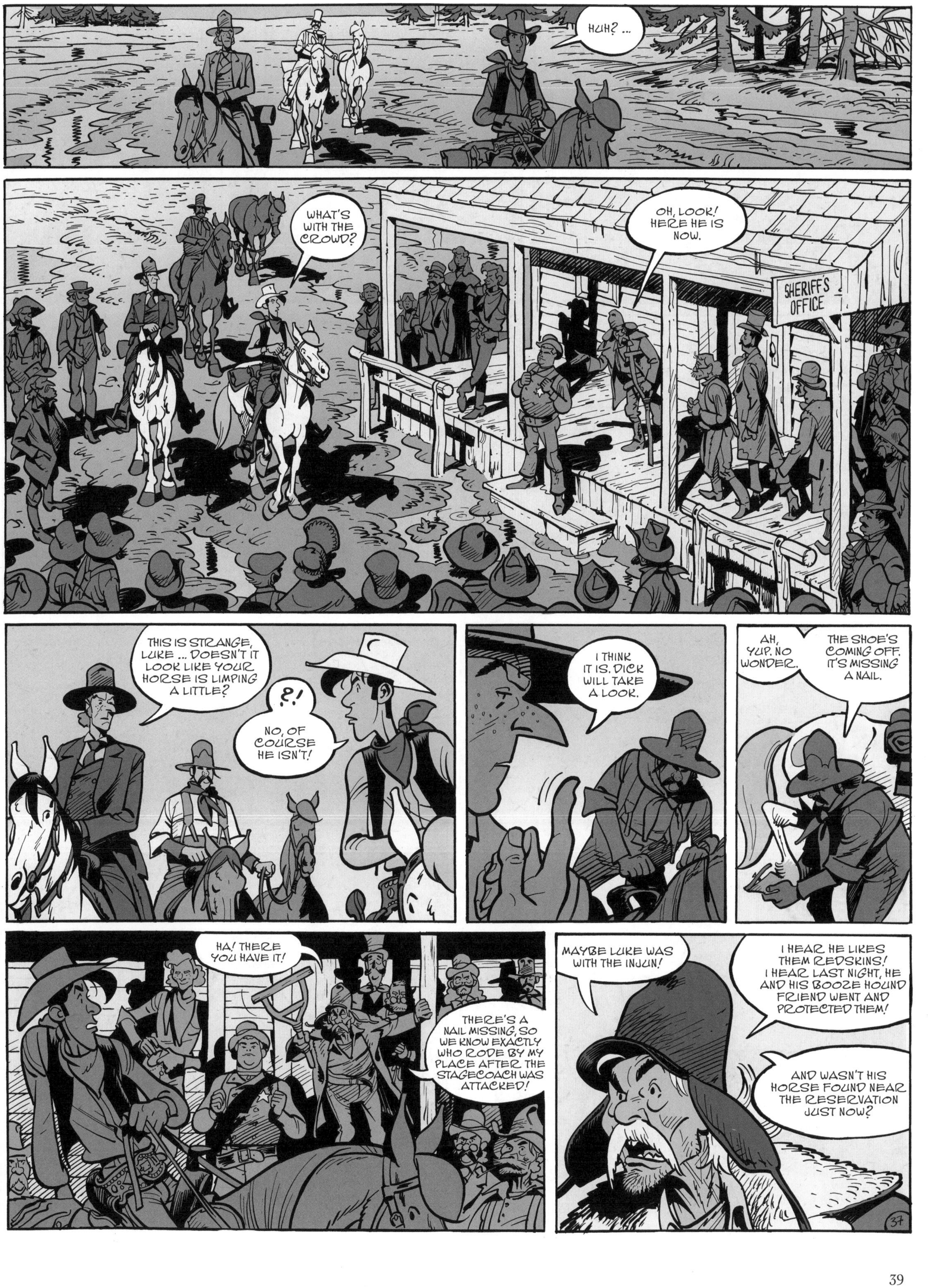
HUH? ...
WHAT'S WITH THE CROWD?
OH, LOOK! HERE HE IS NOW.
SHERIFF'S OFFICE
THIS IS STRANGE, LUKE ... DOESN'T IT LOOK LIKE YOUR HORSE IS LIMPING A LITTLE?
?!
NO, OF COURSE HE ISN'T!
I THINK IT IS. DICK WILL TAKE A LOOK.
AH, YUP. NO WONDER.
THE SHOE'S COMING OFF. IT'S MISSING A NAIL.
HA! THERE YOU HAVE IT!
THERE'S A NAIL MISSING, SO WE KNOW EXACTLY WHO RODE BY MY PLACE AFTER THE STAGECOACH WAS ATTACKED!
MAYBE LUKE WAS WITH THE INJUN!
I HEAR HE LIKES THEM REDSKINS! I HEAR LAST NIGHT, HE AND HIS BOOZE HOUND FRIEND WENT AND PROTECTED THEM!
AND WASN'T HIS HORSE FOUND NEAR THE RESERVATION JUST NOW?
37

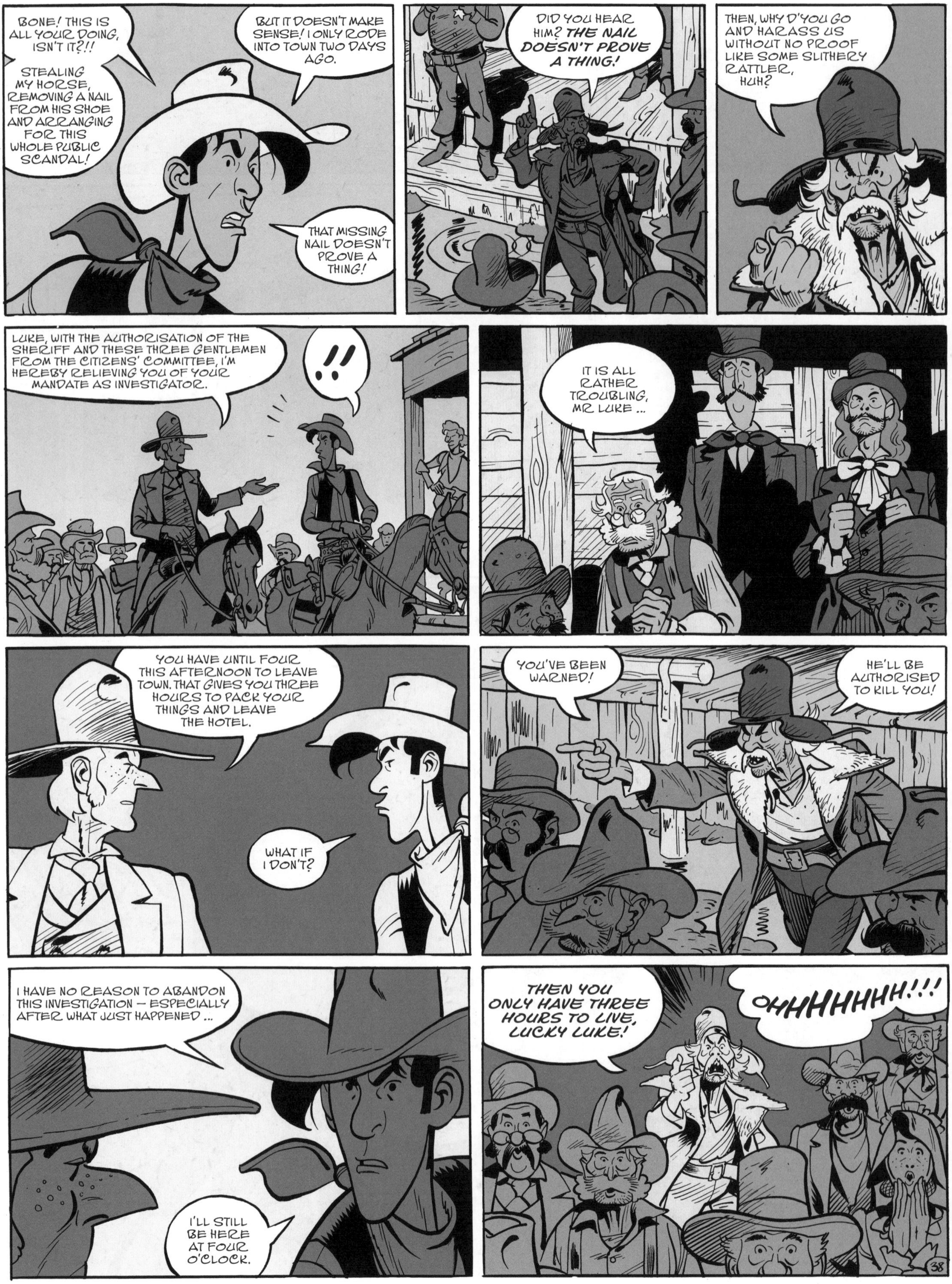

BONE! THIS IS ALL YOUR DOING, ISN'T IT?!!
STEALING MY HORSE, REMOVING A NAIL FROM HIS SHOE AND ARRANGING FOR THIS WHOLE PUBLIC SCANDAL!
BUT IT DOESN'T MAKE SENSE! I ONLY RODE INTO TOWN TWO DAYS AGO.
THAT MISSING NAIL DOESN'T PROVE A THING!
DID YOU HEAR HIM? THE NAIL DOESN'T PROVE A THING!
THEN, WHY D'YOU GO AND HARASS US WITHOUT NO PROOF LIKE SOME SLITHERY RATTLER, HUH?
LUKE, WITH THE AUTHORISATION OF THE SHERIFF AND THESE THREE GENTLEMEN FROM THE CITIZENS' COMMITTEE, I'M HEREBY RELIEVING YOU OF YOUR MANDATE AS INVESTIGATOR.
!!
IT IS ALL RATHER TROUBLING, MR LUKE ...
YOU HAVE UNTIL FOUR THIS AFTERNOON TO LEAVE TOWN. THAT GIVES YOU THREE HOURS TO PACK YOUR THINGS AND LEAVE THE HOTEL.
WHAT IF I DON'T?
YOU'VE BEEN WARNED!
HE'LL BE AUTHORISED TO KILL YOU!
I HAVE NO REASON TO ABANDON THIS INVESTIGATION – ESPECIALLY AFTER WHAT JUST HAPPENED ...
I'LL STILL BE HERE AT FOUR O'CLOCK.
THEN YOU ONLY HAVE THREE HOURS TO LIVE, LUCKY LUKE!
OHHHHHHH!!!
38

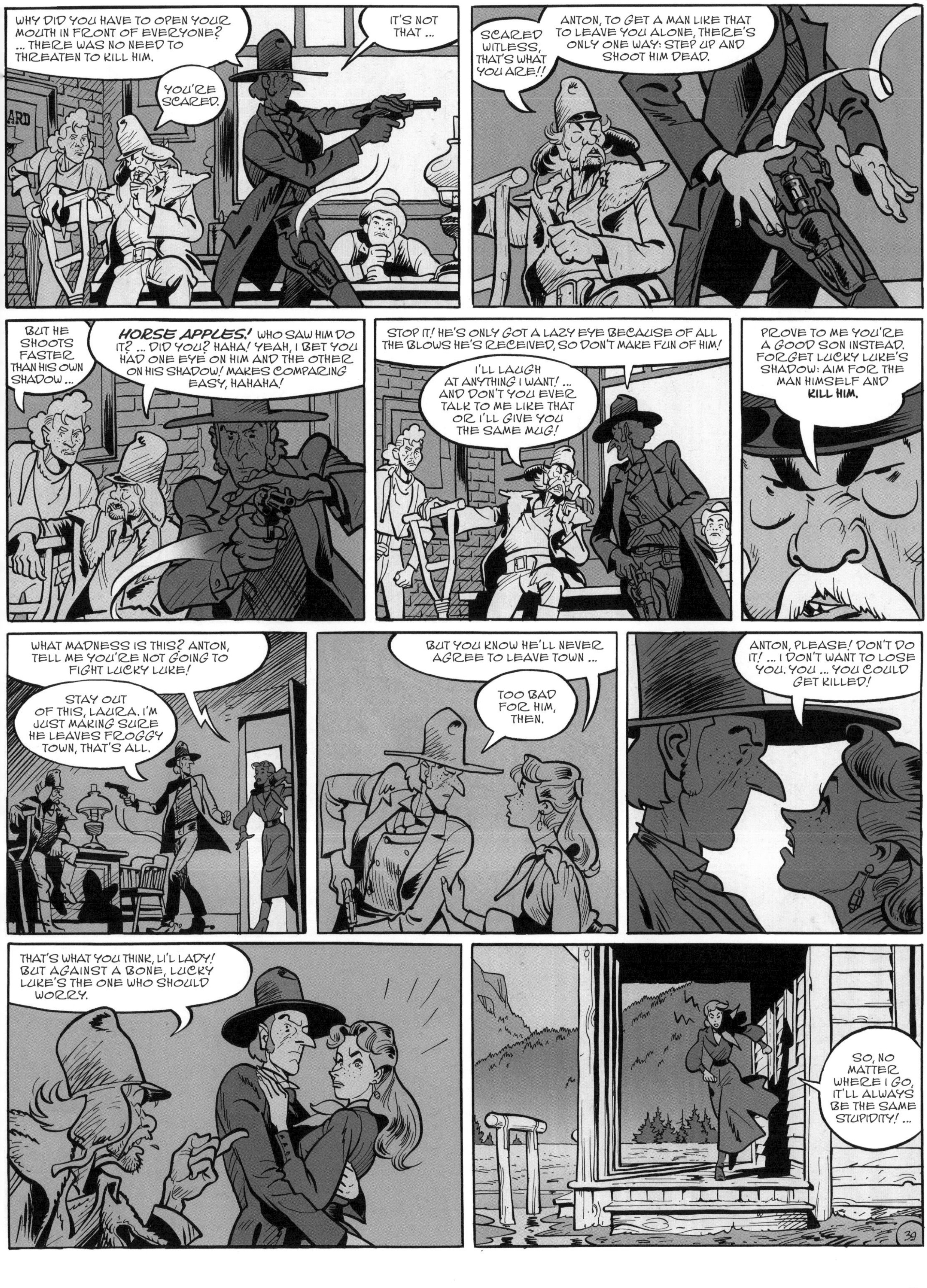

WHY DID YOU HAVE TO OPEN YOUR MOUTH IN FRONT OF EVERYONE? ... THERE WAS NO NEED TO THREATEN TO KILL HIM.
IT'S NOT THAT ...
YOU'RE SCARED.
SCARED WITLESS, THAT'S WHAT YOU ARE!!
ANTON, TO GET A MAN LIKE THAT TO LEAVE YOU ALONE, THERE'S ONLY ONE WAY: STEP UP AND SHOOT HIM DEAD.
BUT HE SHOOTS FASTER THAN HIS OWN SHADOW ...
HORSE APPLES! WHO SAW HIM DO IT? ... DID YOU? HAHA! YEAH, I BET YOU HAD ONE EYE ON HIM AND THE OTHER ON HIS SHADOW! MAKES COMPARING EASY, HAHAHA!
STOP IT! HE'S ONLY GOT A LAZY EYE BECAUSE OF ALL THE BLOWS HE'S RECEIVED, SO DON'T MAKE FUN OF HIM!
I'LL LAUGH AT ANYTHING I WANT! ... AND DON'T YOU EVER TALK TO ME LIKE THAT OR I'LL GIVE YOU THE SAME MUG!
PROVE TO ME YOU'RE A GOOD SON INSTEAD. FORGET LUCKY LUKE'S SHADOW: AIM FOR THE MAN HIMSELF AND KILL HIM.
WHAT MADNESS IS THIS? ANTON, TELL ME YOU'RE NOT GOING TO FIGHT LUCKY LUKE!
STAY OUT OF THIS, LAURA. I'M JUST MAKING SURE HE LEAVES FROGGY TOWN, THAT'S ALL.
BUT YOU KNOW HE'LL NEVER AGREE TO LEAVE TOWN ...
TOO BAD FOR HIM, THEN.
ANTON, PLEASE! DON'T DO IT! ... I DON'T WANT TO LOSE YOU. YOU ... YOU COULD GET KILLED!
THAT'S WHAT YOU THINK, LI'L LADY! BUT AGAINST A BONE, LUCKY LUKE'S THE ONE WHO SHOULD WORRY.
SO, NO MATTER WHERE I GO, IT'LL ALWAYS BE THE SAME STUPIDITY! ...
39

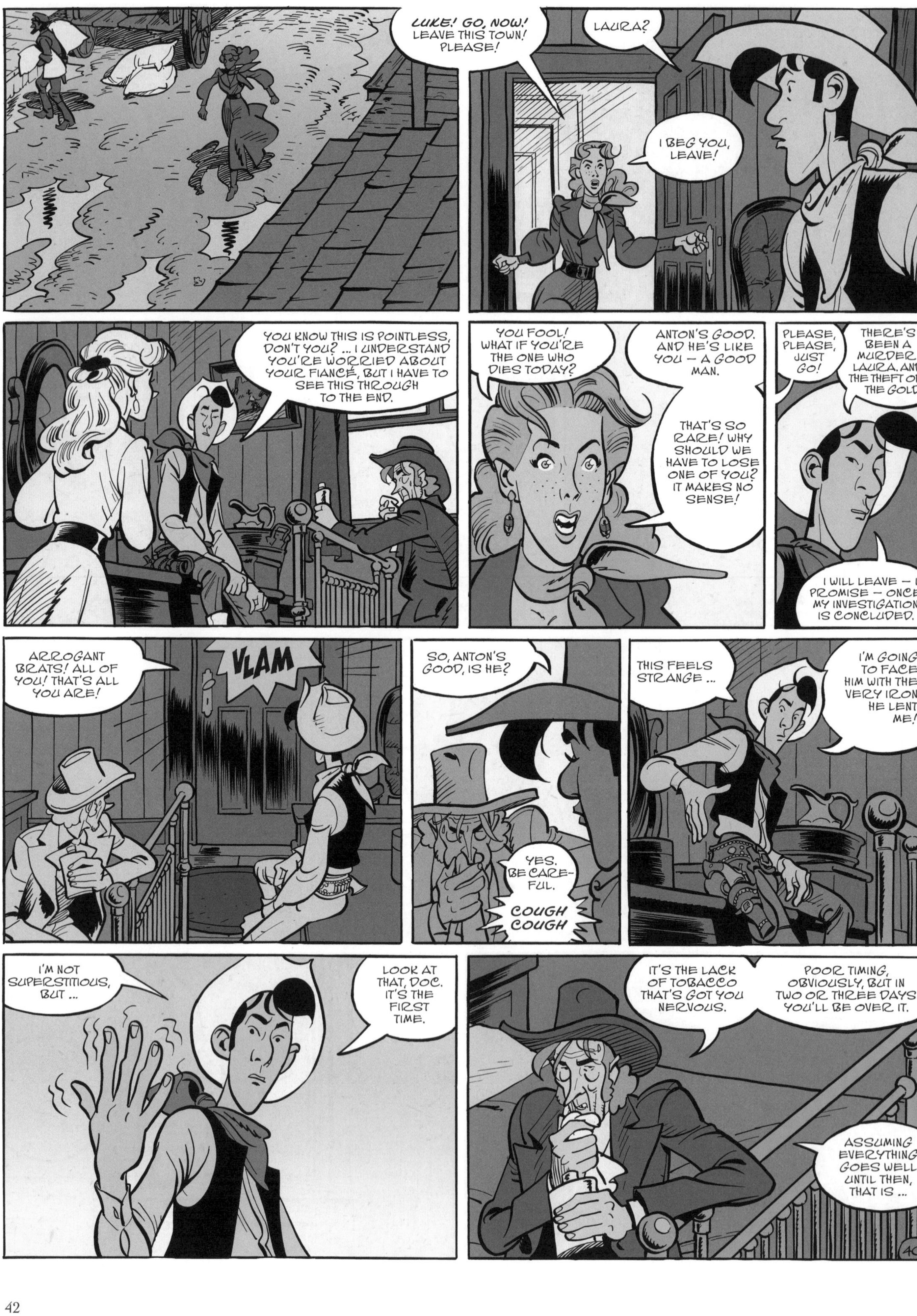

LUKE! GO, NOW! LEAVE THIS TOWN! PLEASE!
LAURA?
I BEG YOU, LEAVE!
YOU KNOW THIS IS POINTLESS, DON'T YOU? ... I UNDERSTAND YOU'RE WORRIED ABOUT YOUR FIANCÉ, BUT I HAVE TO SEE THIS THROUGH TO THE END.
YOU FOOL! WHAT IF YOU'RE THE ONE WHO DIES TODAY?
ANTON'S GOOD. AND HE'S LIKE YOU – A GOOD MAN.
THAT'S SO RARE! WHY SHOULD WE HAVE TO LOSE ONE OF YOU? IT MAKES NO SENSE!
PLEASE, PLEASE, JUST GO!
THERE'S BEEN A MURDER, LAURA, AND THE THEFT OF THE GOLD.
I WILL LEAVE – I PROMISE – ONCE MY INVESTIGATION IS CONCLUDED.
ARROGANT BRATS! ALL OF YOU! THAT'S ALL YOU ARE!
VLAM
SO, ANTON'S GOOD, IS HE?
YES. BE CARE-FUL.
COUGH COUGH
THIS FEELS STRANGE ...
I'M GOING TO FACE HIM WITH THE VERY IRON HE LENT ME!
I'M NOT SUPERSTITIOUS, BUT ...
LOOK AT THAT, DOC. IT'S THE FIRST TIME.
IT'S THE LACK OF TOBACCO THAT'S GOT YOU NERVOUS.
POOR TIMING, OBVIOUSLY, BUT IN TWO OR THREE DAYS YOU'LL BE OVER IT.
ASSUMING EVERYTHING GOES WELL UNTIL THEN, THAT IS ...
40

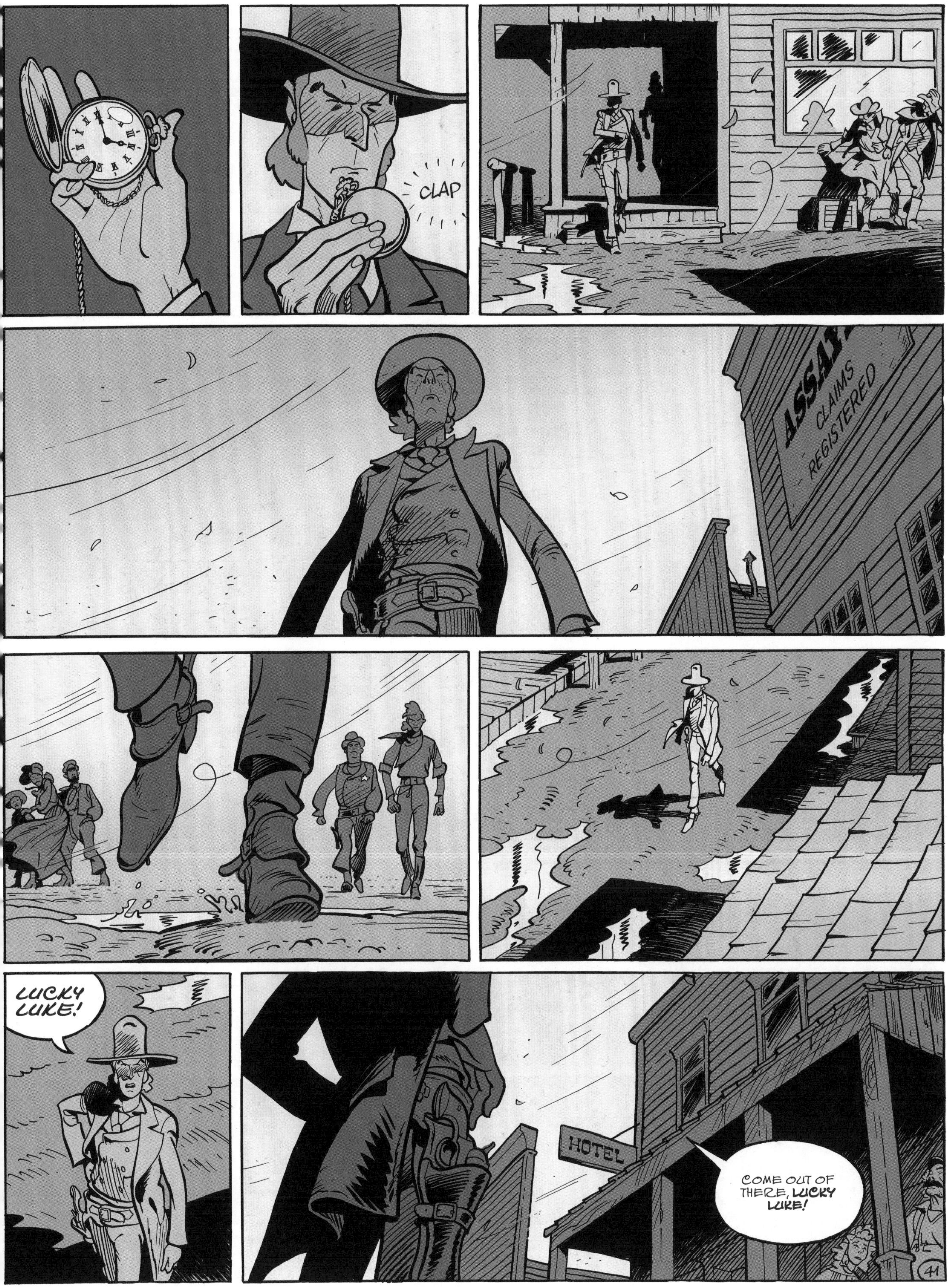

CLAP
ASSAY
CLAIMS
REGISTERED
LUCKY LUKE!
HOTEL
COME OUT OF THERE, LUCKY LUKE!
41

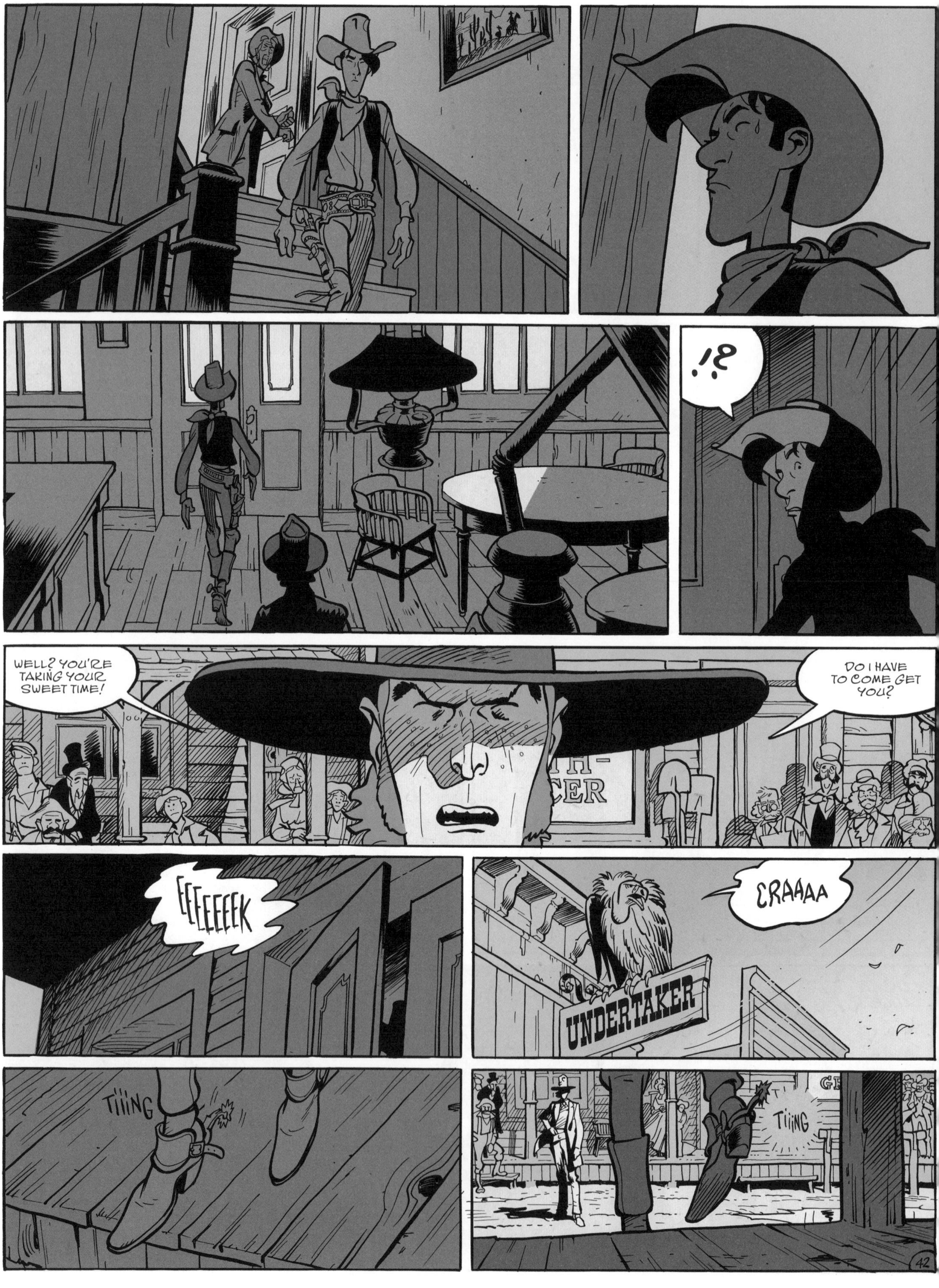
!?
WELL? YOU'RE TAKING YOUR SWEET TIME!
DO I HAVE TO COME GET YOU?
EEEEEEEK
CRAAAA
UNDERTAKER
TiiiNG
TiiNG
42

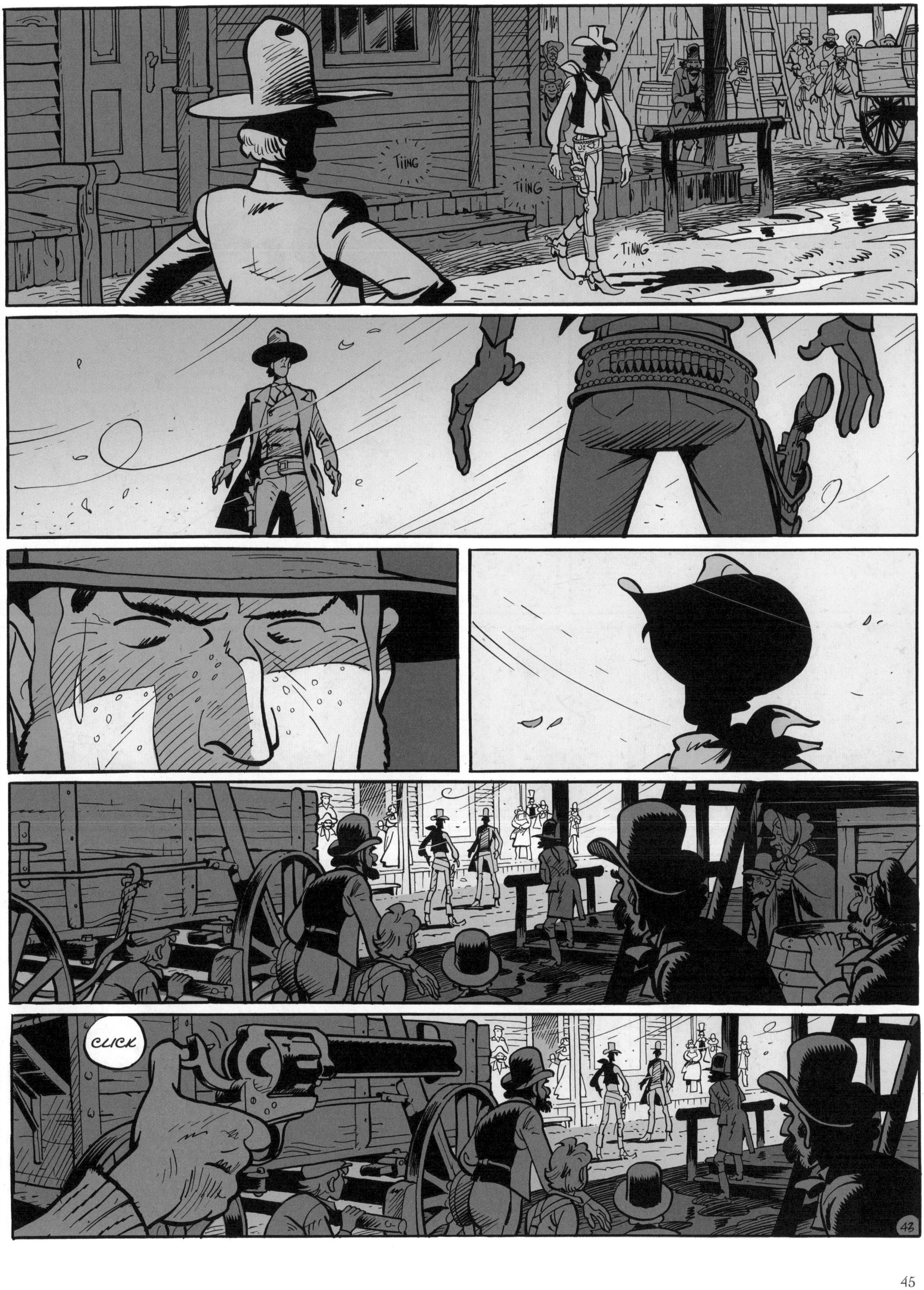
TIING
TIING
TINNG
CLICK
43

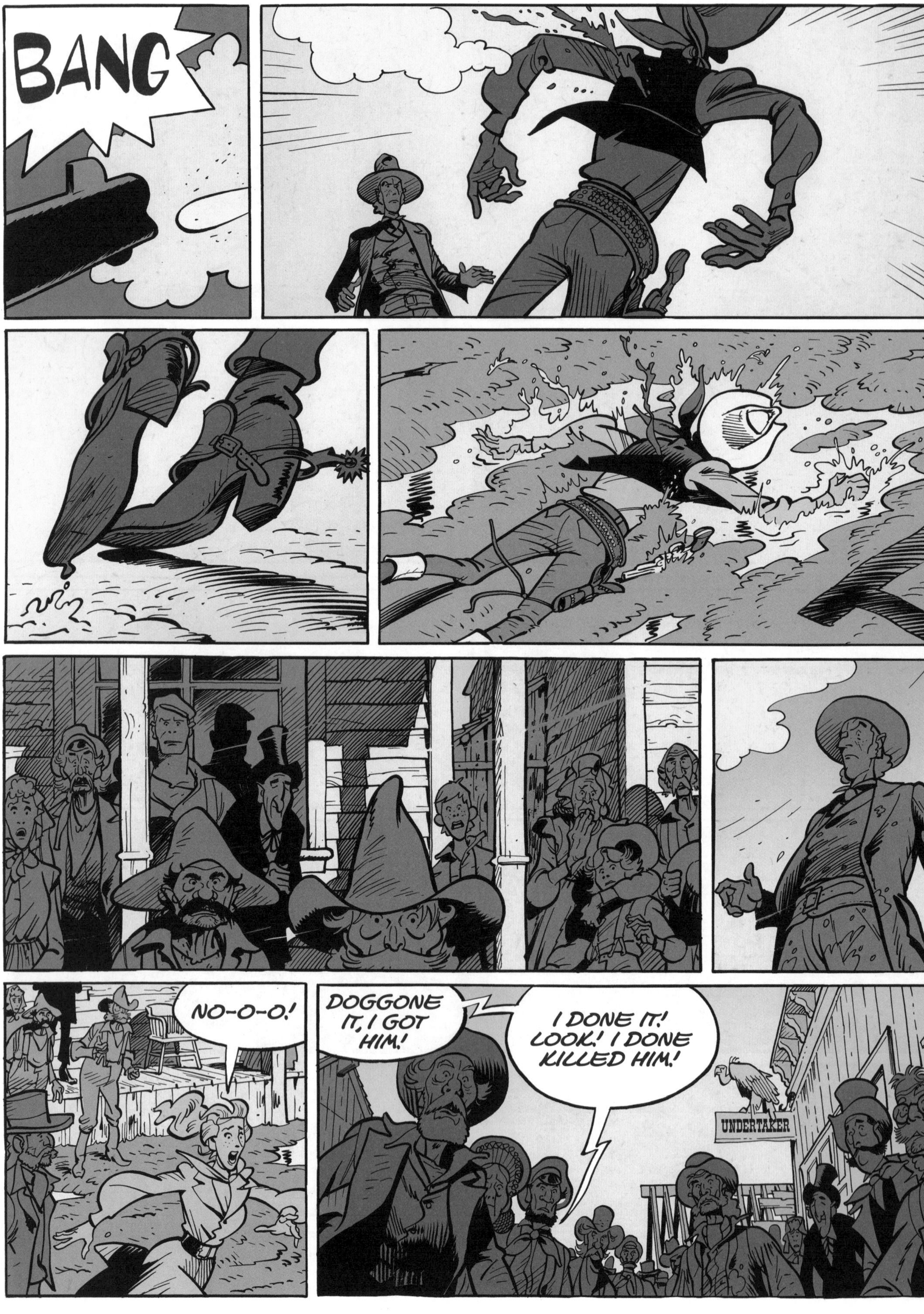
BANG
NO-O-O!
DOGGONE IT, I GOT HIM!
I DONE IT! LOOK! I DONE KILLED HIM!
UNDERTAKER
44

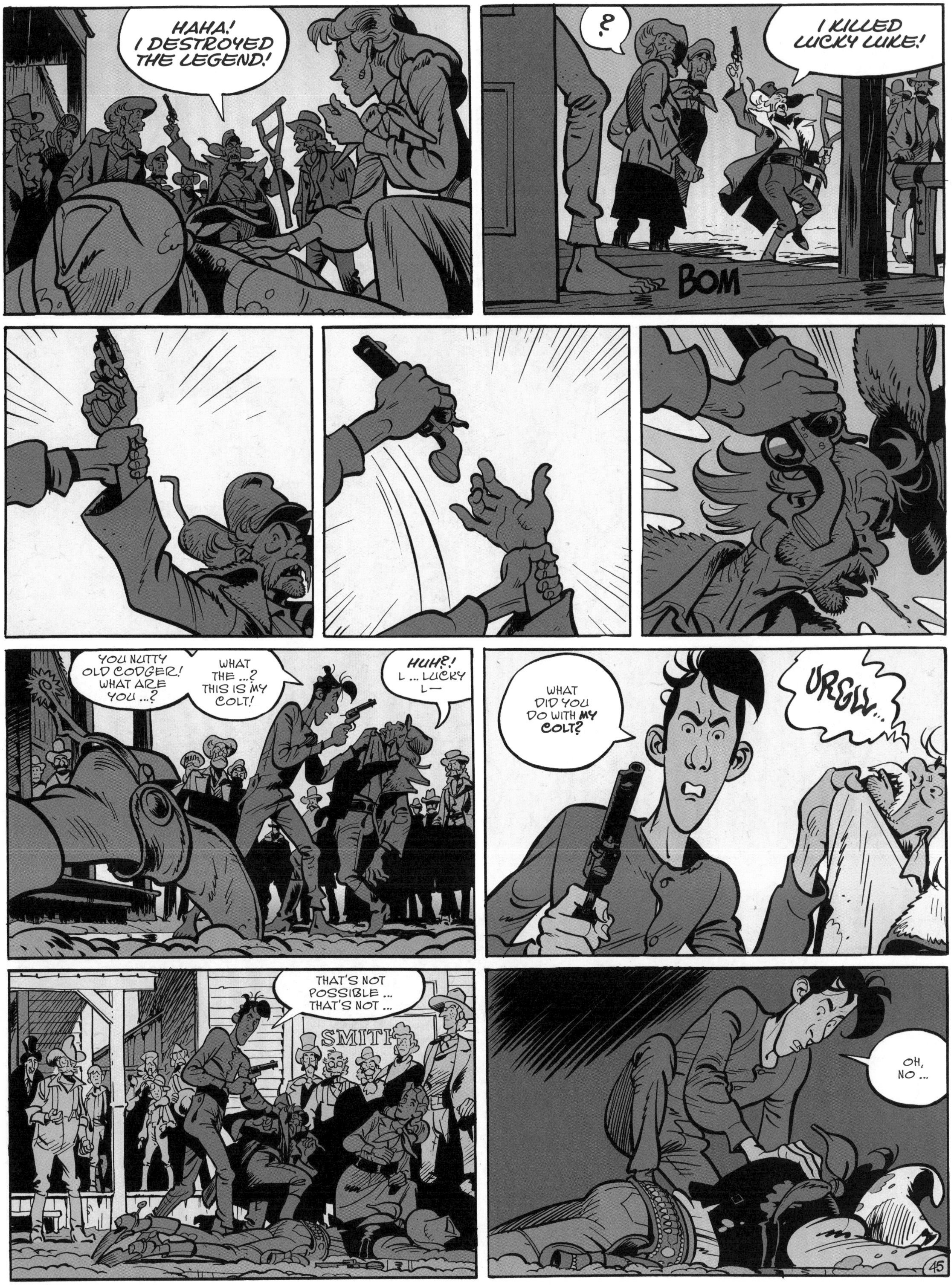
HAHA! I DESTROYED THE LEGEND!
?
I KILLED LUCKY LUKE!
BOM
YOU NUTTY OLD CODGER! WHAT ARE YOU ...?
WHAT THE ...? THIS IS MY COLT!
HUH?! L ... LUCKY L—
WHAT DID YOU DO WITH MY COLT?
URGH...
THAT'S NOT POSSIBLE ... THAT'S NOT ...
SMITH
OH, NO ...
45

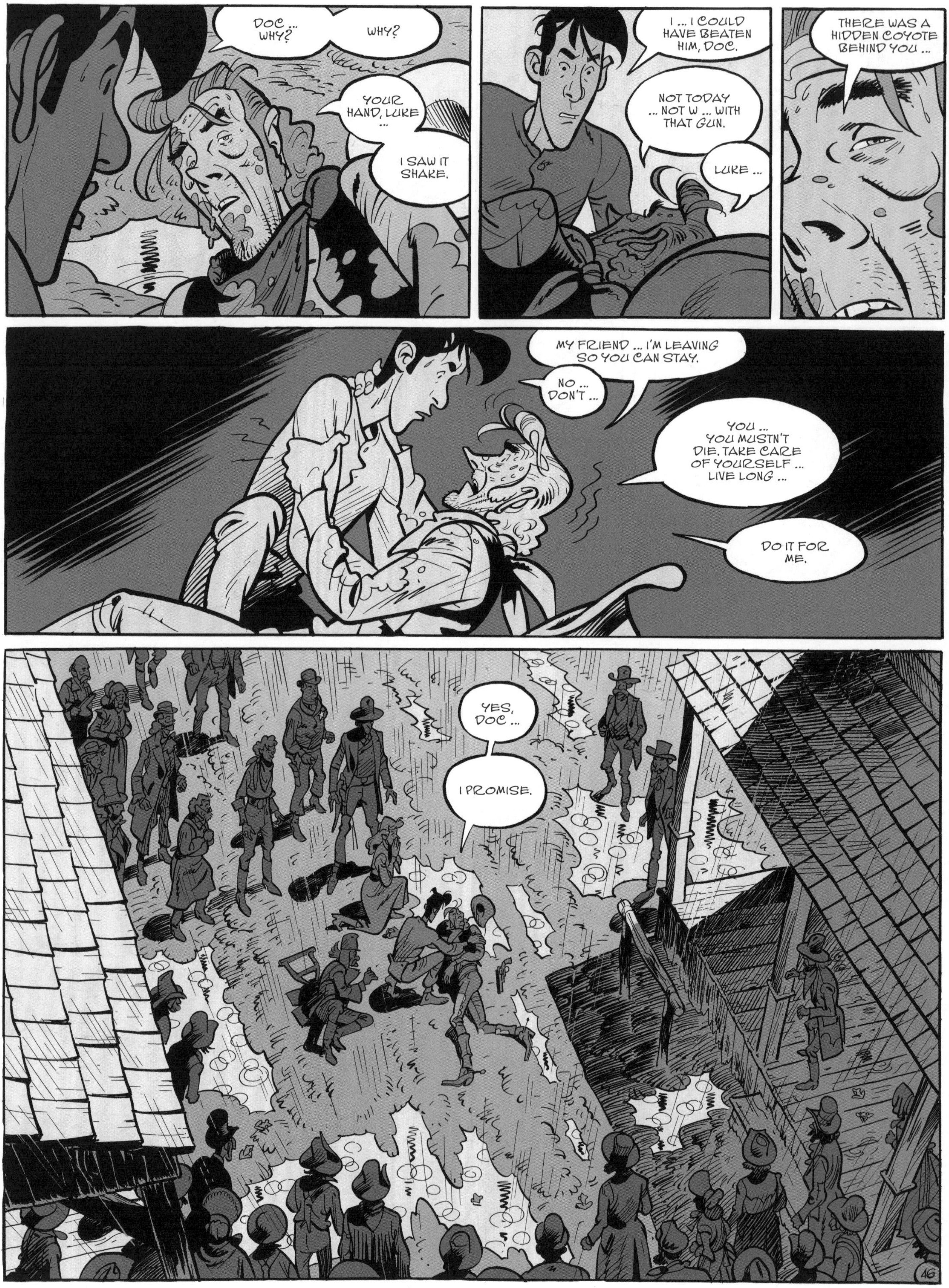
DOC ... WHY?
WHY?
YOUR HAND, LUKE ...
I SAW IT SHAKE.
I ... I COULD HAVE BEATEN HIM, DOC.
NOT TODAY ... NOT W ... WITH THAT GUN.
LUKE ...
THERE WAS A HIDDEN COYOTE BEHIND YOU ...
MY FRIEND ... I'M LEAVING SO YOU CAN STAY.
NO ... DON'T ...
YOU ... YOU MUSTN'T DIE. TAKE CARE OF YOURSELF ... LIVE LONG ...
DO IT FOR ME.
YES, DOC ...
I PROMISE.

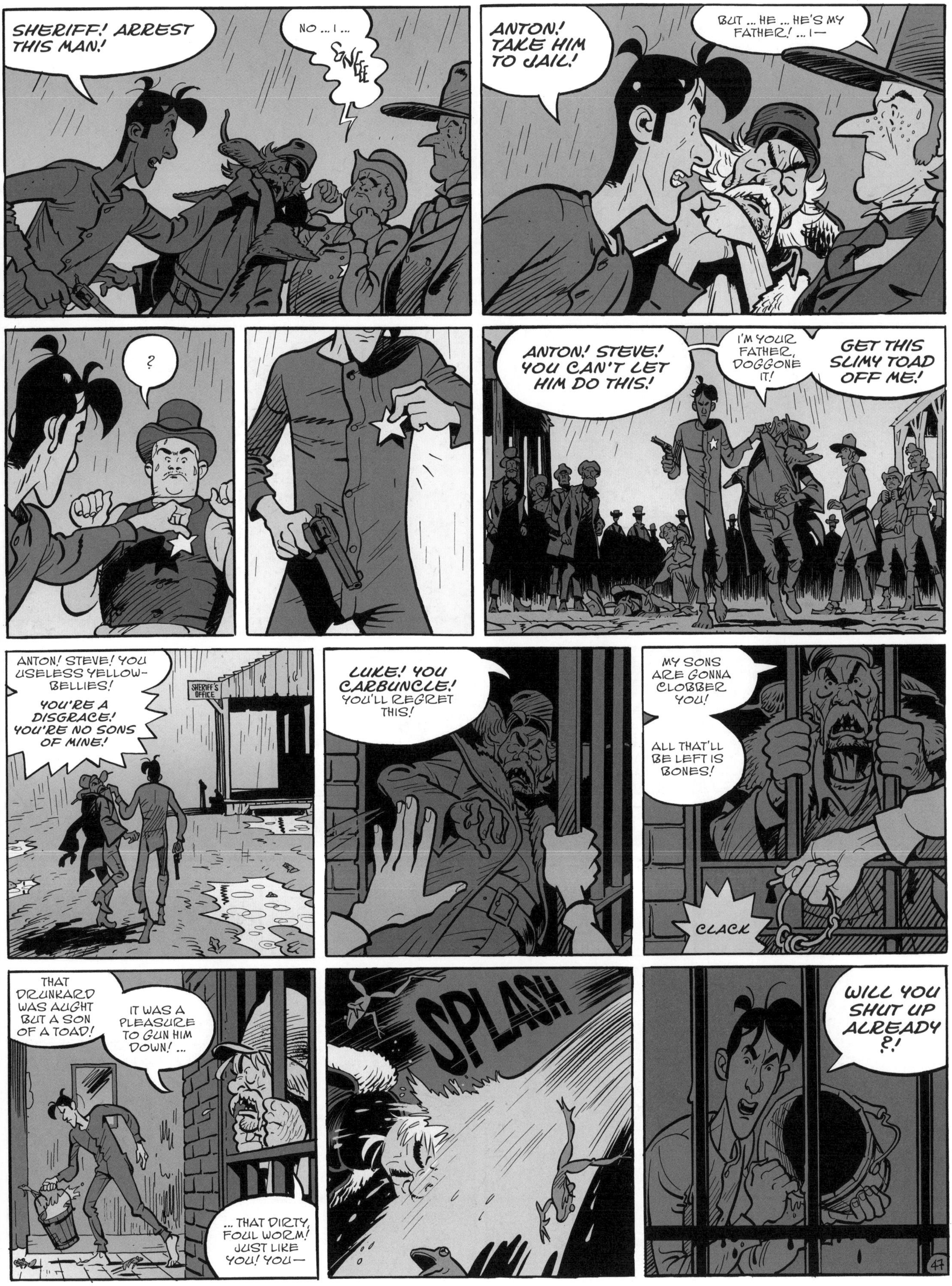
SHERIFF! ARREST THIS MAN!
NO ... I ...
SNEEZE
ANTON! TAKE HIM TO JAIL!
BUT ... HE ... HE'S MY FATHER! ... I—
?
ANTON! STEVE! YOU CAN'T LET HIM DO THIS!
I'M YOUR FATHER, DOGGONE IT!
GET THIS SLIMY TOAD OFF ME!
ANTON! STEVE! YOU USELESS YELLOW-BELLIES!
YOU'RE A DISGRACE! YOU'RE NO SONS OF MINE!
SHERIFF'S OFFICE
LUKE! YOU CARBUNCLE! YOU'LL REGRET THIS!
MY SONS ARE GONNA CLOBBER YOU!
ALL THAT'LL BE LEFT IS BONES!
CLACK
THAT DRUNKARD WAS AUGHT BUT A SON OF A TOAD!
IT WAS A PLEASURE TO GUN HIM DOWN! ...
... THAT DIRTY, FOUL WORM! JUST LIKE YOU! YOU—
SPLASH
WILL YOU SHUT UP ALREADY ?!
47

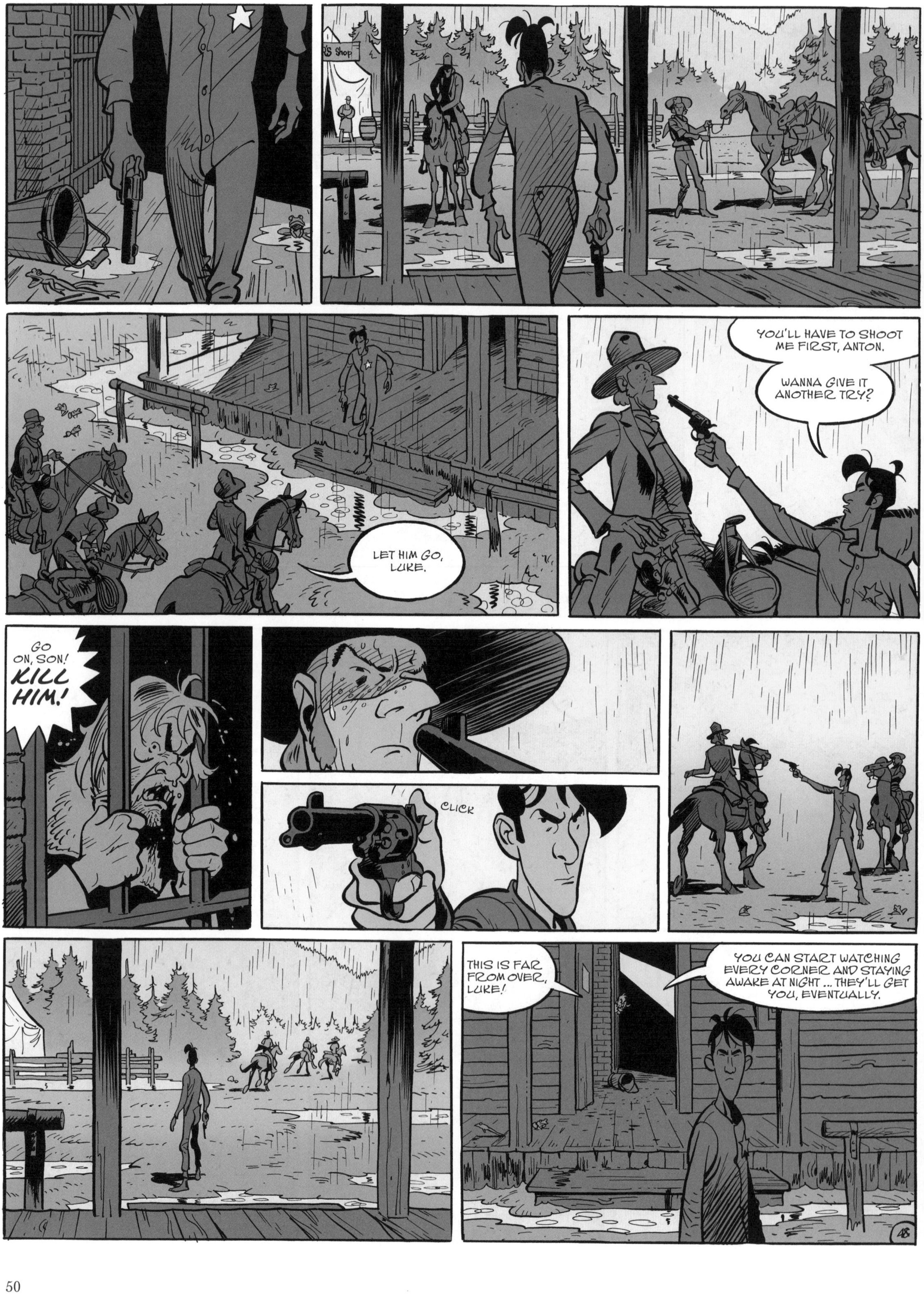

R'S Shop
YOU'LL HAVE TO SHOOT ME FIRST, ANTON.
WANNA GIVE IT ANOTHER TRY?
LET HIM GO, LUKE.
GO ON, SON! KILL HIM!
CLICK
THIS IS FAR FROM OVER, LUKE!
YOU CAN START WATCHING EVERY CORNER AND STAYING AWAKE AT NIGHT ... THEY'LL GET YOU, EVENTUALLY.
48

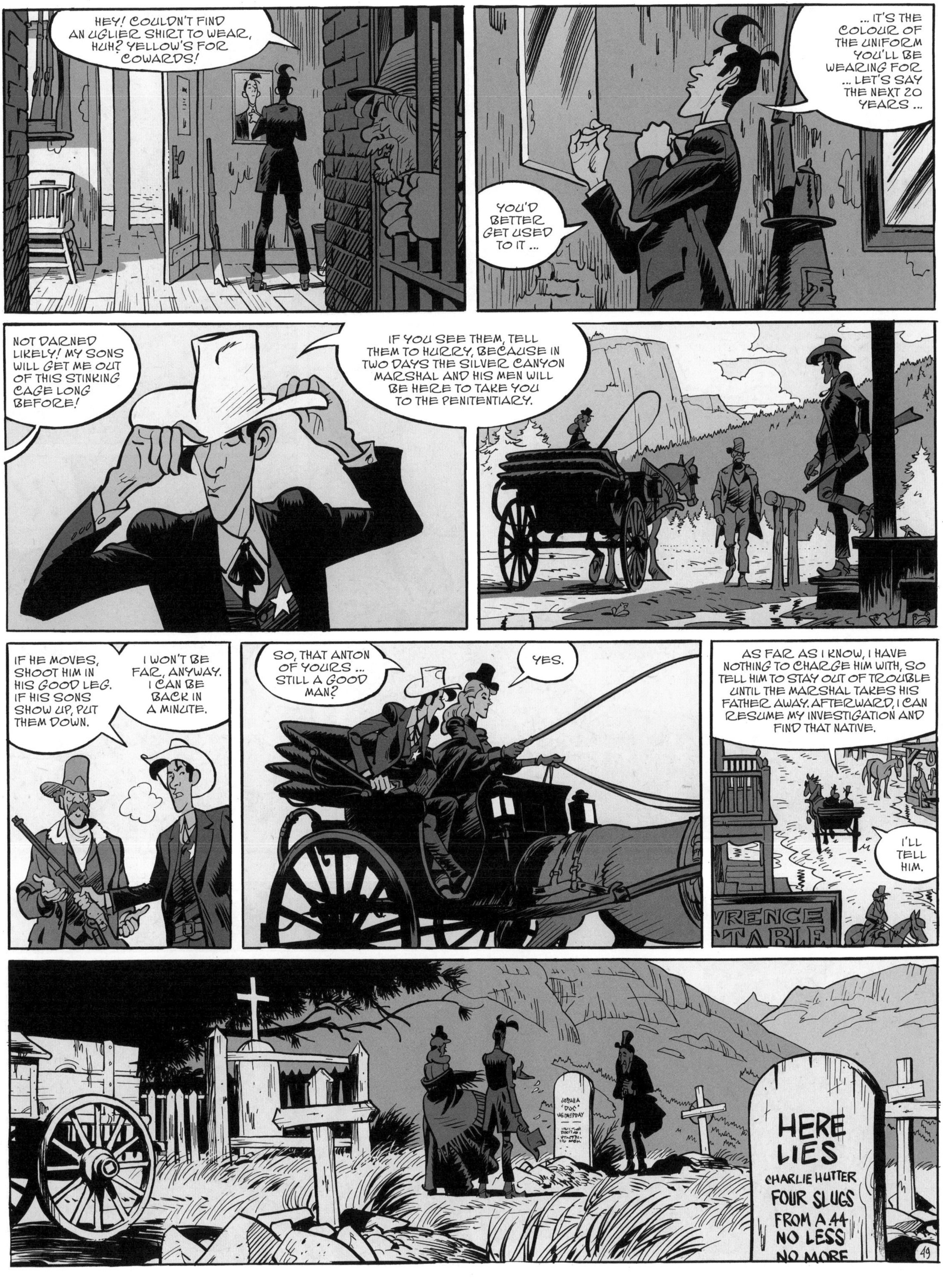
HEY! COULDN'T FIND AN UGLIER SHIRT TO WEAR, HUH? YELLOW'S FOR COWARDS!
... IT'S THE COLOUR OF THE UNIFORM YOU'LL BE WEARING FOR ... LET'S SAY THE NEXT 20 YEARS ...
YOU'D BETTER GET USED TO IT ...
NOT DARNED LIKELY! MY SONS WILL GET ME OUT OF THIS STINKING CAGE LONG BEFORE!
IF YOU SEE THEM, TELL THEM TO HURRY, BECAUSE IN TWO DAYS THE SILVER CANYON MARSHAL AND HIS MEN WILL BE HERE TO TAKE YOU TO THE PENITENTIARY.
IF HE MOVES, SHOOT HIM IN HIS GOOD LEG. IF HIS SONS SHOW UP, PUT THEM DOWN.
I WON'T BE FAR, ANYWAY. I CAN BE BACK IN A MINUTE.
SO, THAT ANTON OF YOURS ... STILL A GOOD MAN?
YES.
AS FAR AS I KNOW, I HAVE NOTHING TO CHARGE HIM WITH, SO TELL HIM TO STAY OUT OF TROUBLE UNTIL THE MARSHAL TAKES HIS FATHER AWAY. AFTERWARD, I CAN RESUME MY INVESTIGATION AND FIND THAT NATIVE.
I'LL TELL HIM.
WRENCE
TABLE
HERE LIES
CHARLIE HUTTER
FOUR SLUGS
FROM A 44
NO LESS
NO MORE
49

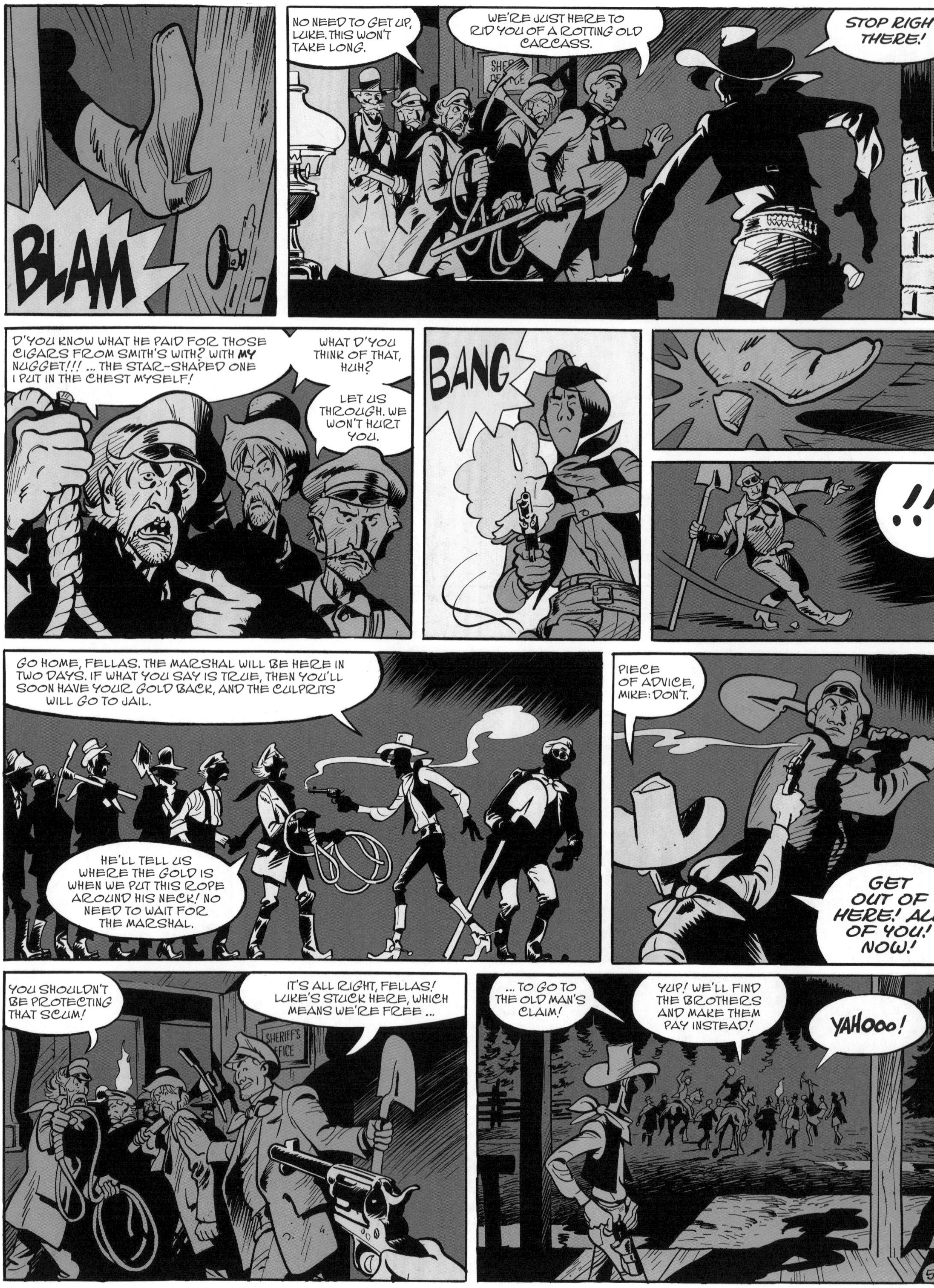
BLAM
NO NEED TO GET UP, LUKE. THIS WON'T TAKE LONG.
WE'RE JUST HERE TO RID YOU OF A ROTTING OLD CARCASS.
STOP RIGHT THERE!
D'YOU KNOW WHAT HE PAID FOR THOSE CIGARS FROM SMITH'S WITH? WITH MY NUGGET!!! ... THE STAR-SHAPED ONE I PUT IN THE CHEST MYSELF!
WHAT D'YOU THINK OF THAT, HUH?
LET US THROUGH. WE WON'T HURT YOU.
BANG
!!
GO HOME, FELLAS. THE MARSHAL WILL BE HERE IN TWO DAYS. IF WHAT YOU SAY IS TRUE, THEN YOU'LL SOON HAVE YOUR GOLD BACK, AND THE CULPRITS WILL GO TO JAIL.
HE'LL TELL US WHERE THE GOLD IS WHEN WE PUT THIS ROPE AROUND HIS NECK! NO NEED TO WAIT FOR THE MARSHAL.
PIECE OF ADVICE, MIKE: DON'T.
GET OUT OF HERE! ALL OF YOU! NOW!
YOU SHOULDN'T BE PROTECTING THAT SCUM!
IT'S ALL RIGHT, FELLAS! LUKE'S STUCK HERE, WHICH MEANS WE'RE FREE ...
SHERIFF'S OFFICE
... TO GO TO THE OLD MAN'S CLAIM!
YUP! WE'LL FIND THE BROTHERS AND MAKE THEM PAY INSTEAD!
YAHOOO!
50

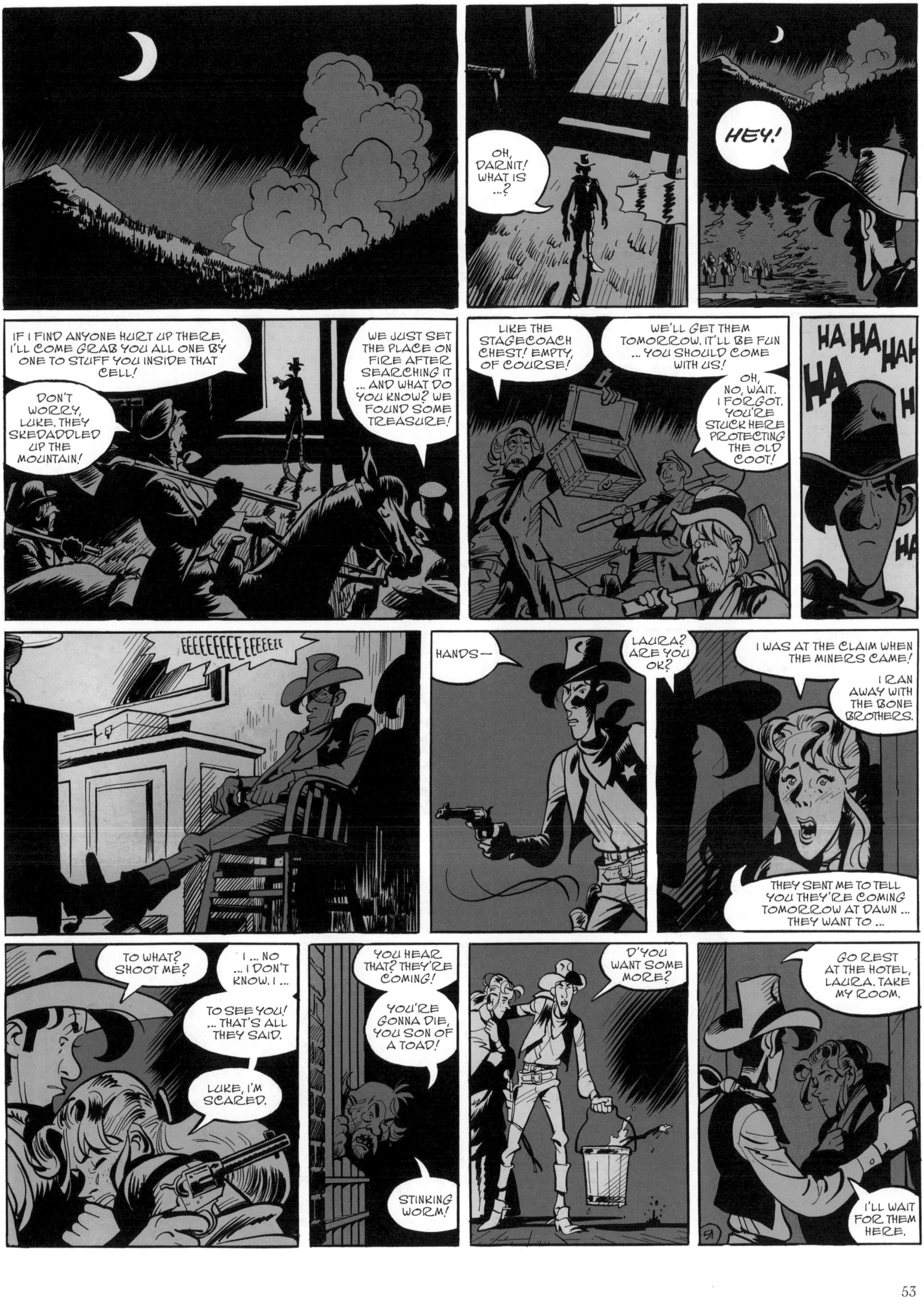
OH, DARNIT! WHAT IS ...?
HEY!
IF I FIND ANYONE HURT UP THERE, I'LL COME GRAB YOU ALL ONE BY ONE TO STUFF YOU INSIDE THAT CELL!
DON'T WORRY, LUKE. THEY SKEDADDLED UP THE MOUNTAIN!
WE JUST SET THE PLACE ON FIRE AFTER SEARCHING IT ... AND WHAT DO YOU KNOW? WE FOUND SOME TREASURE!
LIKE THE STAGECOACH CHEST! EMPTY, OF COURSE!
WE'LL GET THEM TOMORROW. IT'LL BE FUN ... YOU SHOULD COME WITH US!
OH, NO, WAIT. I FORGOT. YOU'RE STUCK HERE PROTECTING THE OLD COOT!
HA HA HA HAH HA H HA
EEEEEEEEEEEEEEEE
HANDS—
LAURA? ARE YOU OK?
I WAS AT THE CLAIM WHEN THE MINERS CAME!
I RAN AWAY WITH THE BONE BROTHERS.
THEY SENT ME TO TELL YOU THEY'RE COMING TOMORROW AT DAWN ... THEY WANT TO ...
TO WHAT? SHOOT ME?
I ... NO ... I DON'T KNOW. I ...
TO SEE YOU! ... THAT'S ALL THEY SAID.
LUKE, I'M SCARED.
YOU HEAR THAT? THEY'RE COMING!
YOU'RE GONNA DIE, YOU SON OF A TOAD!
STINKING WORM!
D'YOU WANT SOME MORE?
GO REST AT THE HOTEL, LAURA. TAKE MY ROOM.
I'LL WAIT FOR THEM HERE.

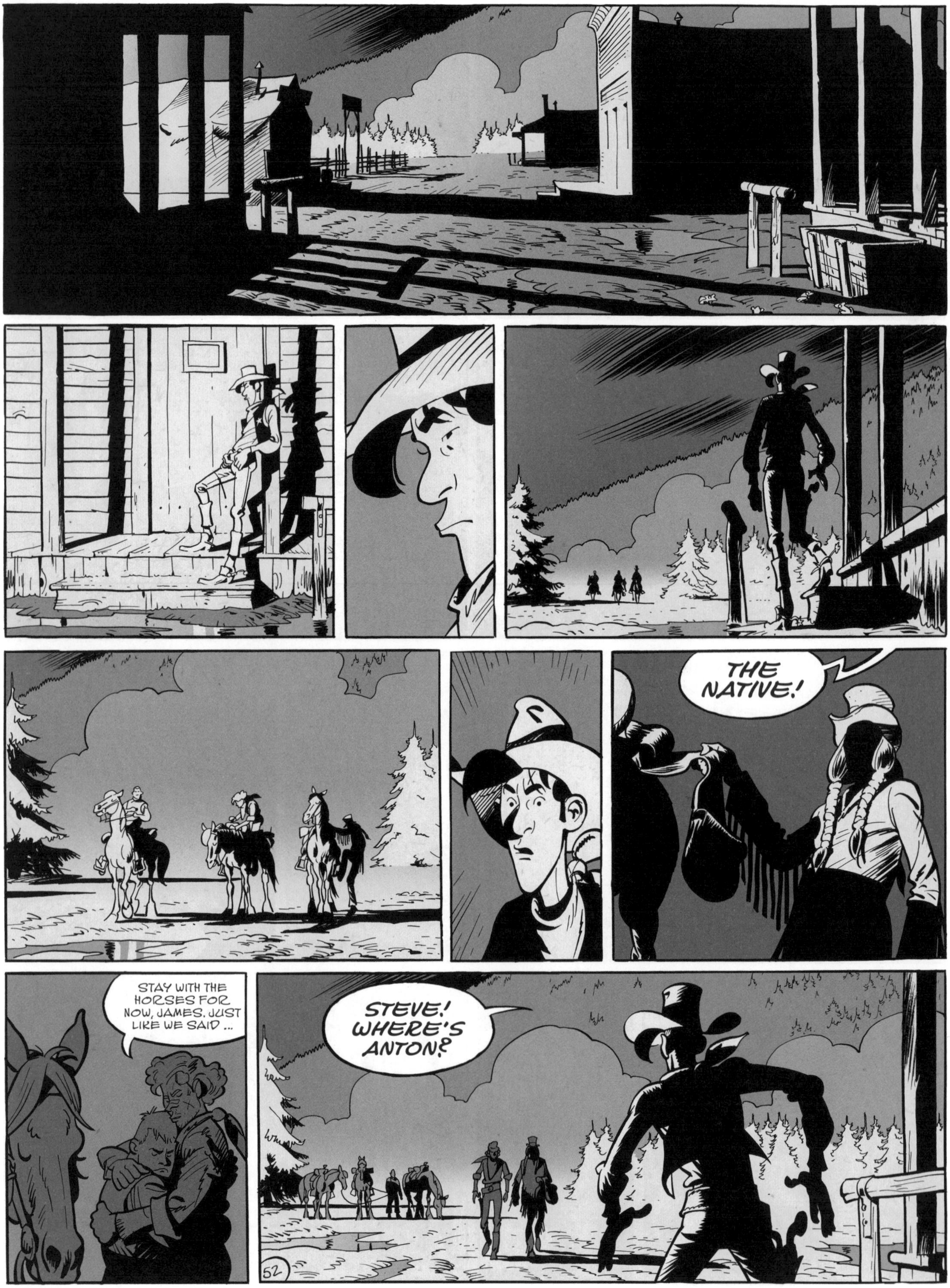
THE NATIVE!
STAY WITH THE HORSES FOR NOW, JAMES. JUST LIKE WE SAID ...
STEVE! WHERE'S ANTON?
52

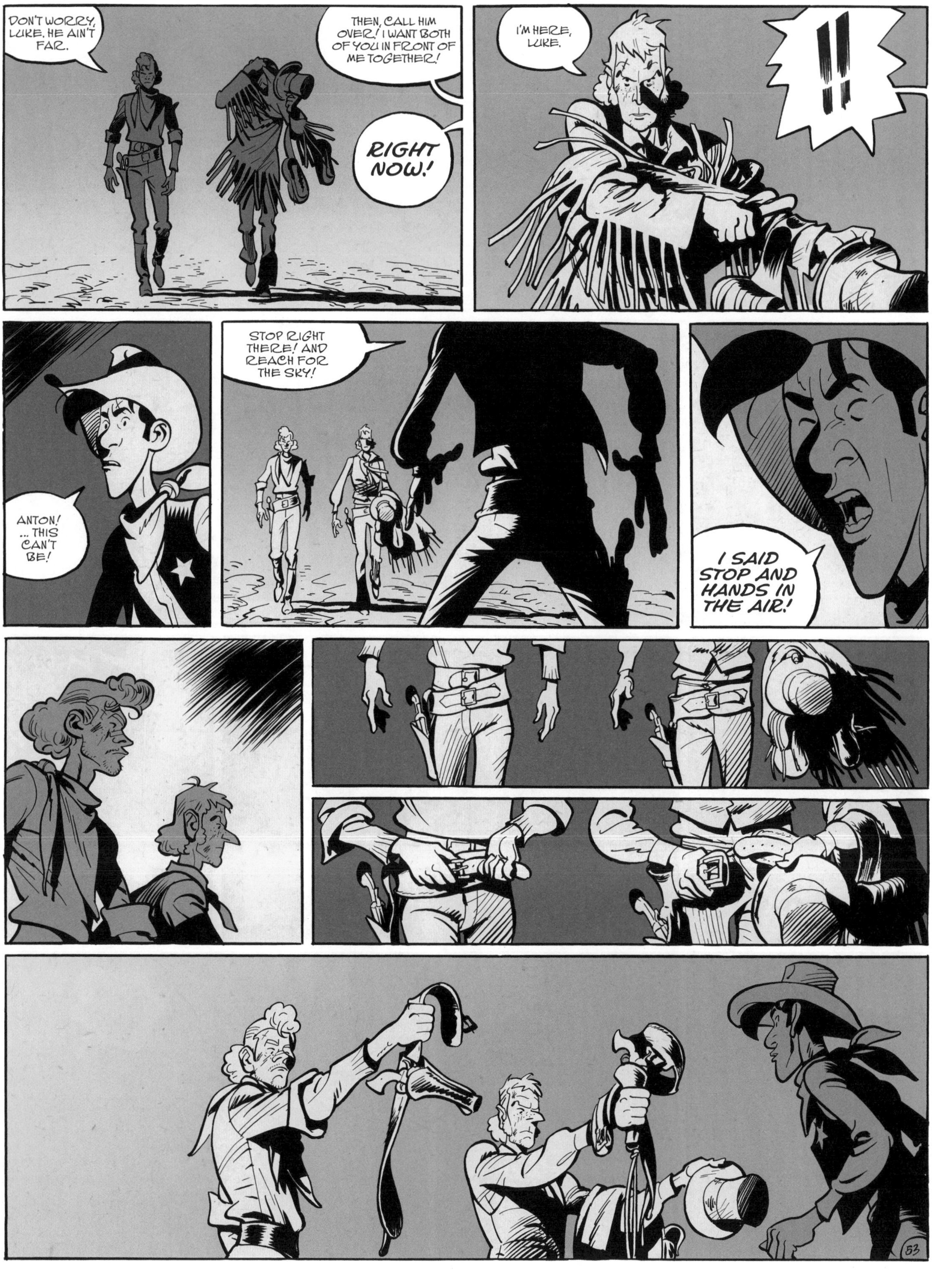
DON'T WORRY, LUKE. HE AIN'T FAR.
THEN, CALL HIM OVER! I WANT BOTH OF YOU IN FRONT OF ME TOGETHER!
RIGHT NOW!
I'M HERE, LUKE.
!!
ANTON! ... THIS CAN'T BE!
STOP RIGHT THERE! AND REACH FOR THE SKY!
I SAID STOP AND HANDS IN THE AIR!
53

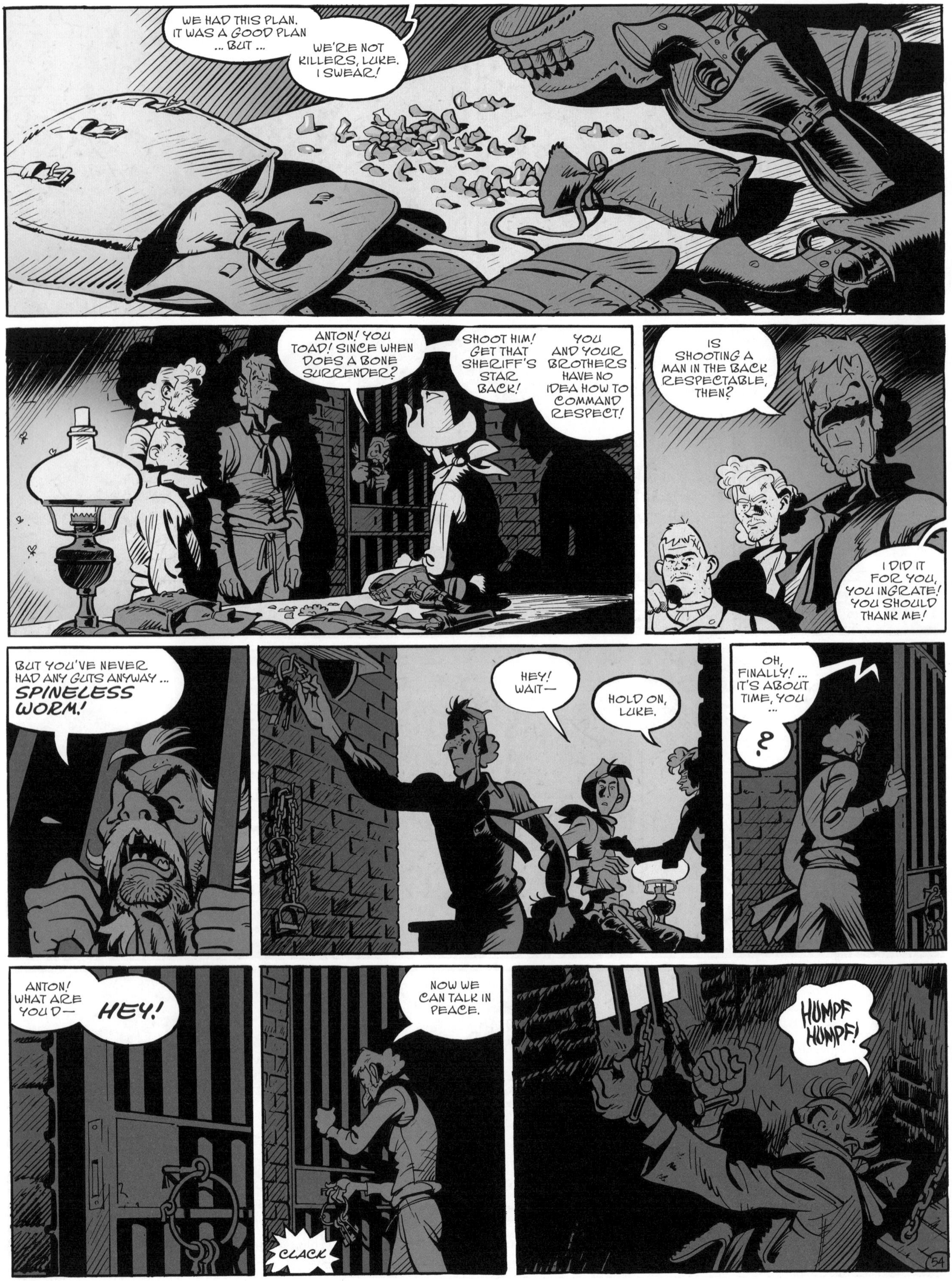
WE HAD THIS PLAN. IT WAS A GOOD PLAN ... BUT ...
WE'RE NOT KILLERS, LUKE. I SWEAR!
ANTON! YOU TOAD! SINCE WHEN DOES A BONE SURRENDER?
SHOOT HIM! GET THAT SHERIFF'S STAR BACK!
YOU AND YOUR BROTHERS HAVE NO IDEA HOW TO COMMAND RESPECT!
IS SHOOTING A MAN IN THE BACK RESPECTABLE, THEN?
I DID IT FOR YOU, YOU INGRATE! YOU SHOULD THANK ME!
BUT YOU'VE NEVER HAD ANY GUTS ANYWAY ... SPINELESS WORM!
HEY! WAIT—
HOLD ON, LUKE.
OH, FINALLY! ... IT'S ABOUT TIME, YOU ...
?
ANTON! WHAT ARE YOU D—
HEY!
NOW WE CAN TALK IN PEACE.
CLACK
HUMPF HUMPF!
54

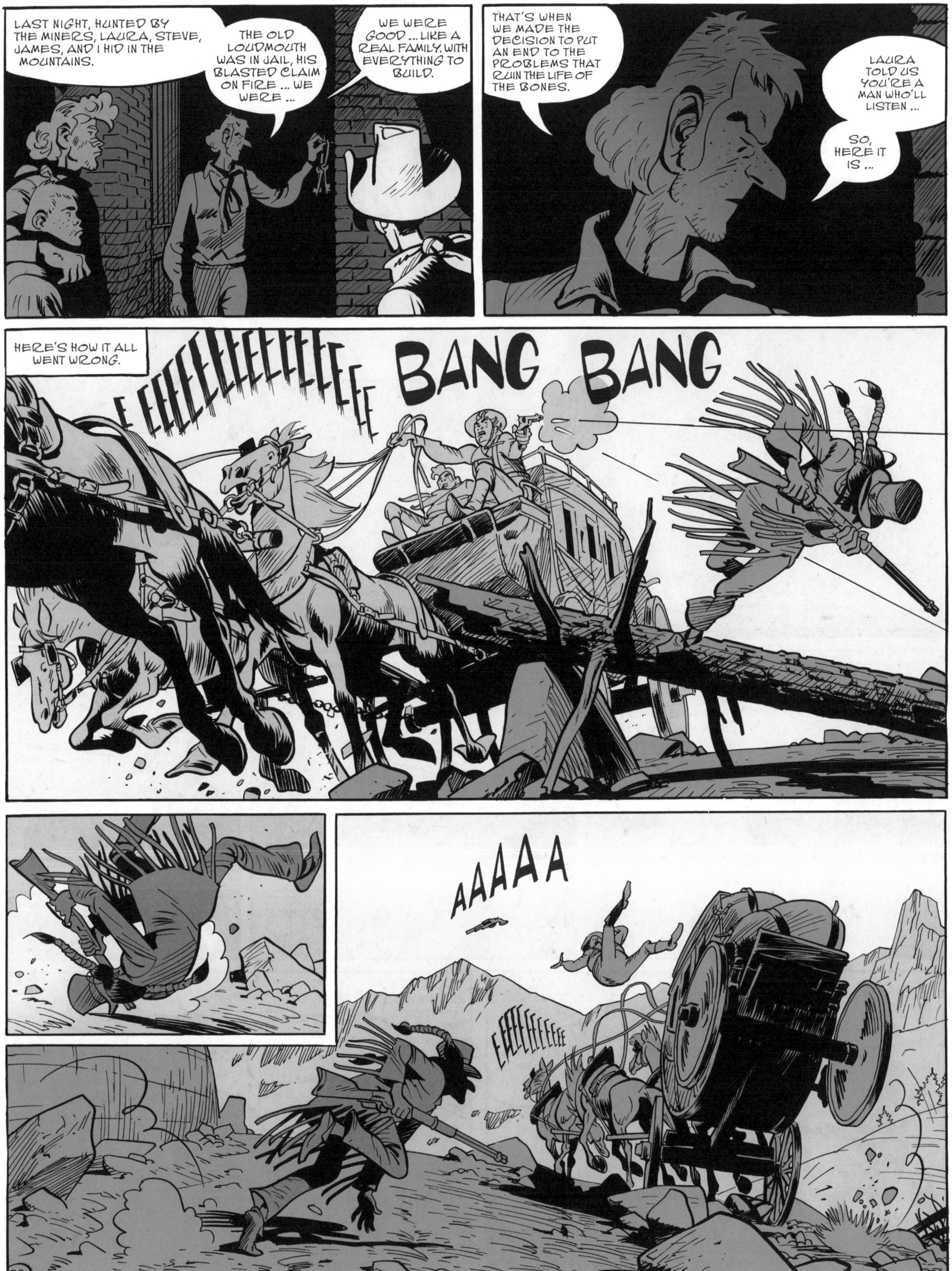

LAST NIGHT, HUNTED BY THE MINERS, LAURA, STEVE, JAMES, AND I HID IN THE MOUNTAINS.
THE OLD LOUDMOUTH WAS IN JAIL, HIS BLASTED CLAIM ON FIRE ... WE WERE ...
WE WERE GOOD ... LIKE A REAL FAMILY. WITH EVERYTHING TO BUILD.
THAT'S WHEN WE MADE THE DECISION TO PUT AN END TO THE PROBLEMS THAT RUIN THE LIFE OF THE BONES.
LAURA TOLD US YOU'RE A MAN WHO'LL LISTEN ...
SO, HERE IT IS ...
HERE'S HOW IT ALL WENT WRONG.
EEEEEEEEEEEEEEEEE
BANG
BANG
AAAAA
EEEEEEEEEEE
55

GET UP!

YOU, UP THERE, BRING THAT CHEST DOWN AND TIE IT TO MY SADDLE. MAKE IT TIGHT.

YES, YES.

BRUMPF

STEVE! DON'T DO IT!

DON'T TOUCH THAT CHEST, DARNIT!

HE'S GONNA SHOOT YOU, BOB! I HAVE TO.

JUST DRAW! AND SHOOT HIM IN HIS FEATHERED HAT!

GET BACK.

?!

WAIT A MINUTE! WHERE HAVE I SEEN THAT UGLY MUG BEF—

I SAID GET BACK!

GO ON! STEP BACK!

HOLY MOSES! ANTON?! YOU FILTHY CUSS!

WAIT ... THAT MEANS STEVE ... HE'S ALSO ...

STINKING BROTHERS! ROTTEN FAMILY! JUST WAIT UNTIL THE OTHERS HEAR ABOUT THIS!

NO! ... BOB, YOU CAN'T TELL ANYONE!

IT'S JUST US THREE HERE ... WE ... COME ON, WE'LL SPLIT IT ...

ARE YOU KIDDING?! NEVER!

YOU'LL HAVE TO SHOOT ME IF YOU WANT ME TO SHUT UP!

BE REASONABLE, BOB ... WE DON'T WANT TO SHOOT YOU!

56

THEN POINT THAT RIFLE SOMEWHERE ELSE.

FIRST, SWEAR YOU WON'T SAY A THING!

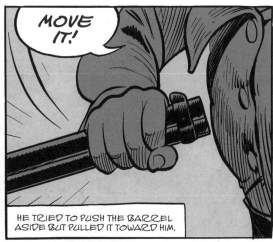

MOVE IT!

HE TRIED TO PUSH THE BARREL ASIDE BUT PULLED IT TOWARD HIM.

MY FINGER WAS ON THE TRIGGER.

THE BULLET WENT RIGHT THROUGH BOB'S HEART.

BLAM

IT ... IT WAS AN ACCIDENT!

I'D TAKEN THE OLD MAN'S HORSE. LESS RECOGNISABLE. I DIDN'T EVEN TRY TO ERASE MY TRACKS AS I BROUGHT IT BACK.

WHY BOTHER, WHEN I'D BE THE ONE WHO'D GO LOOKING FOR THAT PHANTOM INDIAN? ...

THERE. YOU'VE GOT THE GOLD, THE CULPRITS ...

... AND OUR LIVES IN YOUR HANDS.

I BELIEVE YOU ...

... AND I BELIEVE IN JUSTICE.

TOMORROW, THE MARSHAL WILL BE TAKING YOUR FATHER TO THE PENITENTIARY. YOU'LL GO WITH HIM BACK TO SILVER CANYON AND HE'LL HAND YOU OVER TO THE JUDGE.

YOU'LL BE CARRYING A LETTER FROM ME, IN WHICH I'LL WRITE THAT YOU TURNED YOURSELVES IN IN GOOD FAITH.

YOU'LL PROBABLY GO TO PRISON, BUT YOU SHOULDN'T STAY THERE FOR TOO LONG, AND—

THANK YOU, LUCKY LUKE!

57

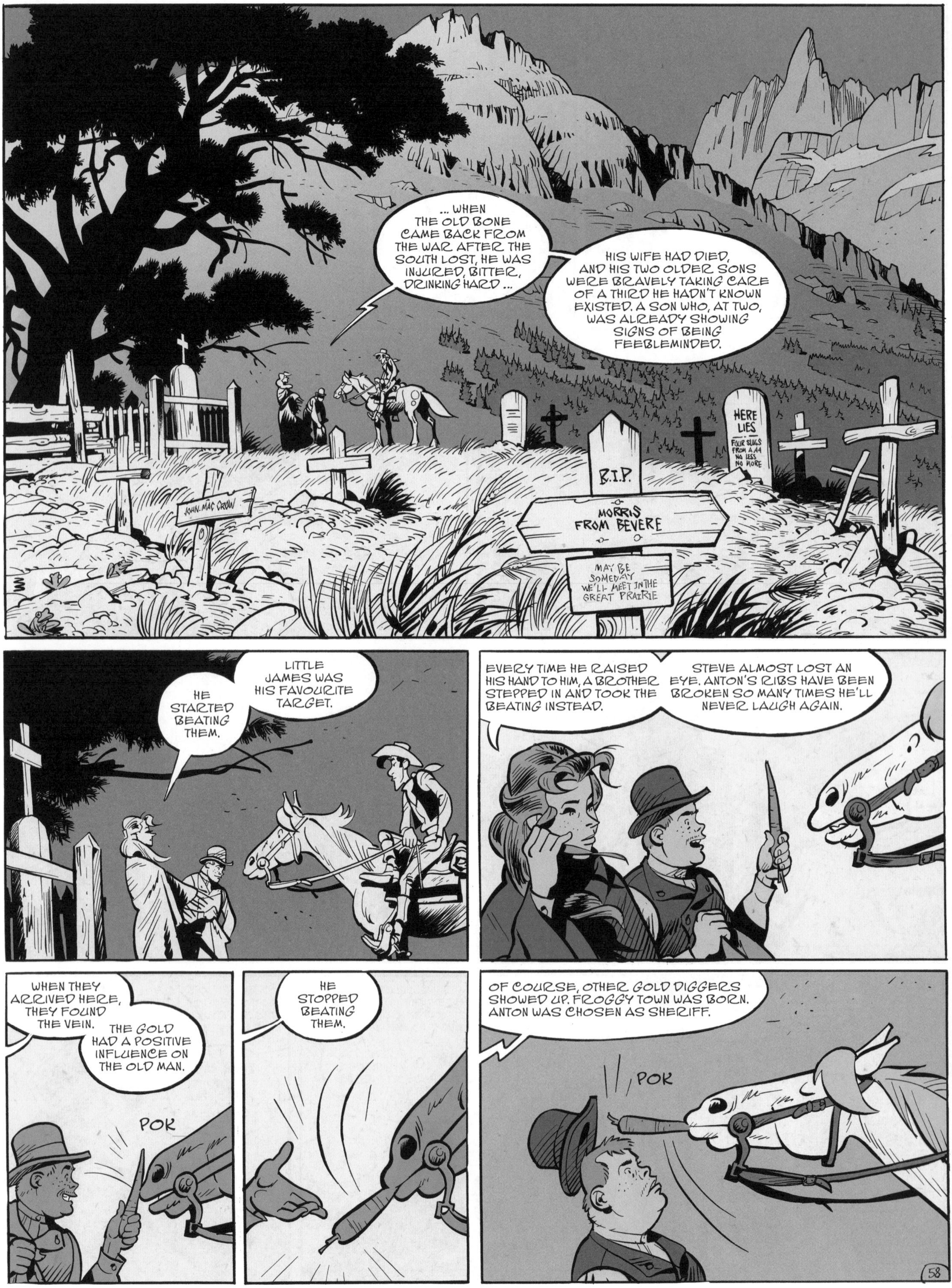
... WHEN THE OLD BONE CAME BACK FROM THE WAR AFTER THE SOUTH LOST, HE WAS INJURED, BITTER, DRINKING HARD ...
HIS WIFE HAD DIED, AND HIS TWO OLDER SONS WERE BRAVELY TAKING CARE OF A THIRD HE HADN'T KNOWN EXISTED. A SON WHO, AT TWO, WAS ALREADY SHOWING SIGNS OF BEING FEEBLEMINDED.
HERE LIES
FOUR SLUGS FROM A 44 NO LESS NO MORE
R.I.P.
JOHN MAC CROW
MORRIS FROM BEVERE
MAY BE SOMEDAY WE'LL MEET IN THE GREAT PRAIRIE
HE STARTED BEATING THEM.
LITTLE JAMES WAS HIS FAVOURITE TARGET.
EVERY TIME HE RAISED HIS HAND TO HIM, A BROTHER STEPPED IN AND TOOK THE BEATING INSTEAD.
STEVE ALMOST LOST AN EYE. ANTON'S RIBS HAVE BEEN BROKEN SO MANY TIMES HE'LL NEVER LAUGH AGAIN.
WHEN THEY ARRIVED HERE, THEY FOUND THE VEIN.
THE GOLD HAD A POSITIVE INFLUENCE ON THE OLD MAN.
POK
HE STOPPED BEATING THEM.
OF COURSE, OTHER GOLD DIGGERS SHOWED UP. FROGGY TOWN WAS BORN. ANTON WAS CHOSEN AS SHERIFF.
POK
58

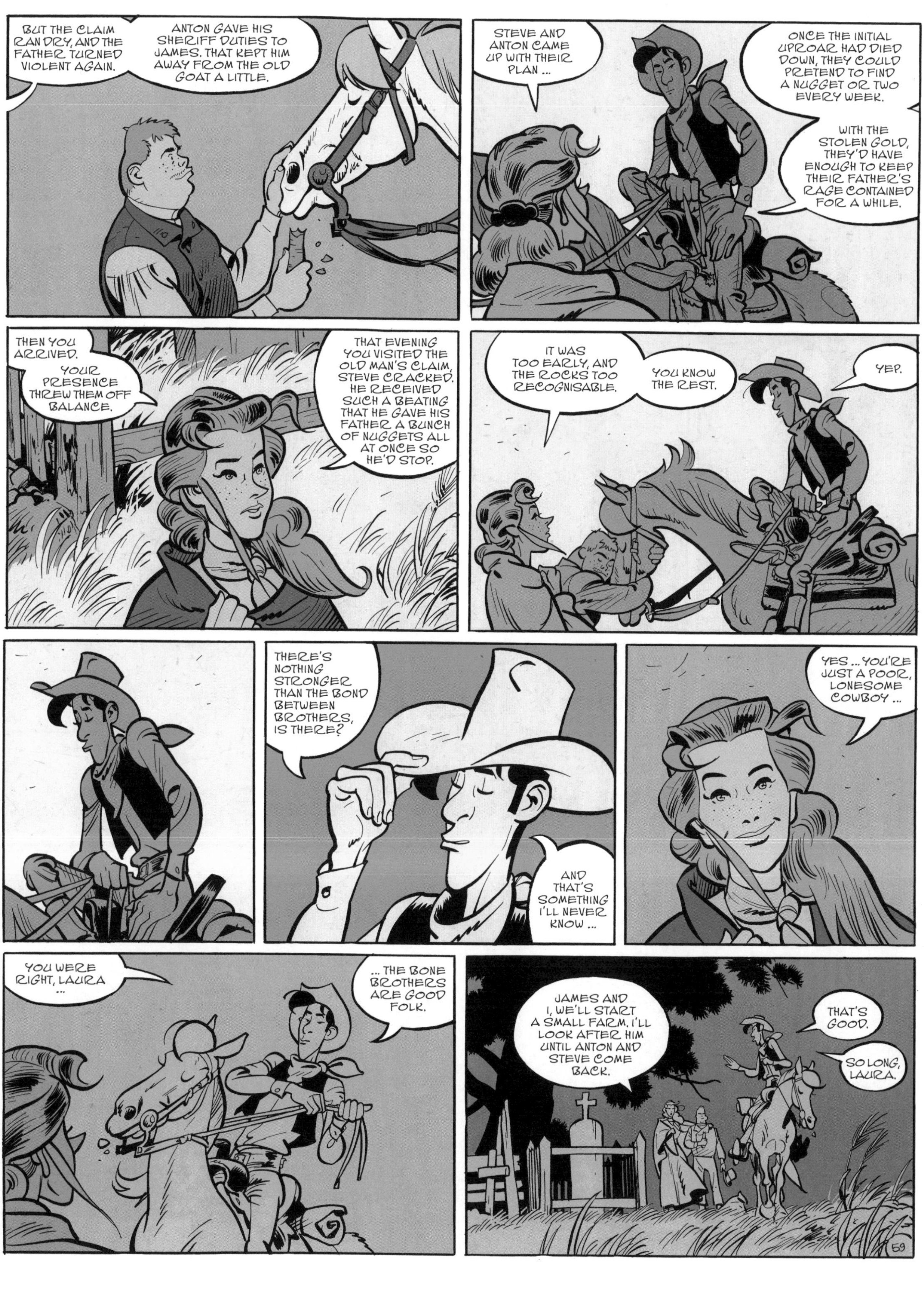
BUT THE CLAIM RAN DRY, AND THE FATHER TURNED VIOLENT AGAIN.
ANTON GAVE HIS SHERIFF DUTIES TO JAMES. THAT KEPT HIM AWAY FROM THE OLD GOAT A LITTLE.
STEVE AND ANTON CAME UP WITH THEIR PLAN ...
ONCE THE INITIAL UPROAR HAD DIED DOWN, THEY COULD PRETEND TO FIND A NUGGET OR TWO EVERY WEEK.
WITH THE STOLEN GOLD, THEY'D HAVE ENOUGH TO KEEP THEIR FATHER'S RAGE CONTAINED FOR A WHILE.
THEN YOU ARRIVED.
YOUR PRESENCE THREW THEM OFF BALANCE.
THAT EVENING YOU VISITED THE OLD MAN'S CLAIM, STEVE CRACKED. HE RECEIVED SUCH A BEATING THAT HE GAVE HIS FATHER A BUNCH OF NUGGETS ALL AT ONCE SO HE'D STOP.
IT WAS TOO EARLY, AND THE ROCKS TOO RECOGNISABLE.
YOU KNOW THE REST.
YEP.
THERE'S NOTHING STRONGER THAN THE BOND BETWEEN BROTHERS, IS THERE?
AND THAT'S SOMETHING I'LL NEVER KNOW ...
YES ... YOU'RE JUST A POOR, LONESOME COWBOY ...
YOU WERE RIGHT, LAURA ...
... THE BONE BROTHERS ARE GOOD FOLK.
JAMES AND I, WE'LL START A SMALL FARM. I'LL LOOK AFTER HIM UNTIL ANTON AND STEVE COME BACK.
THAT'S GOOD.
SO LONG, LAURA.
59

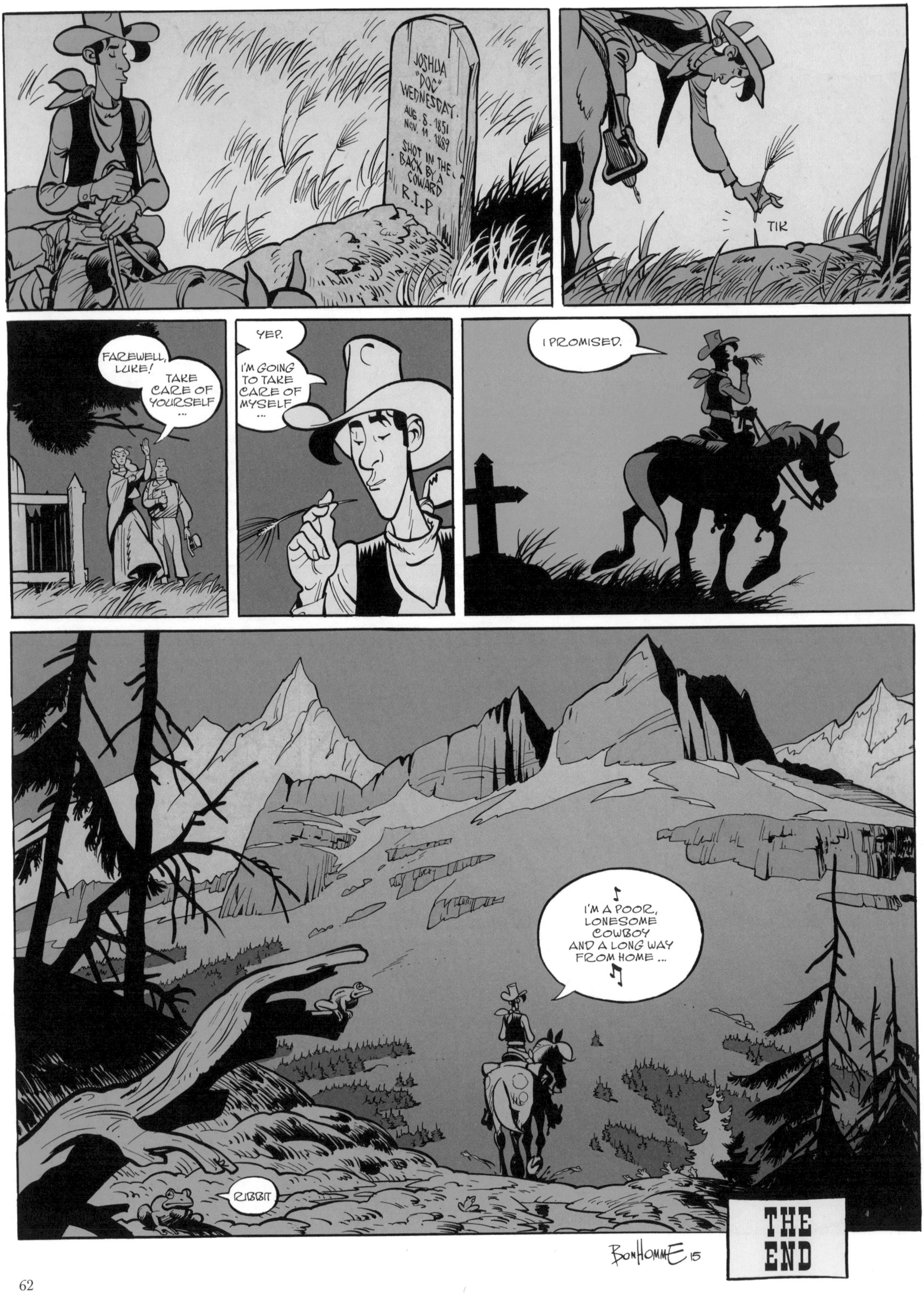
JOSHUA "DOC" WEDNESDAY. AUG. 5. 1851 NOV. 11. 1889 SHOT IN THE BACK BY A COWARD R.I.P
TIK
FAREWELL, LUKE!
TAKE CARE OF YOURSELF ...
YEP.
I'M GOING TO TAKE CARE OF MYSELF ...
I PROMISED.
I'M A POOR, LONESOME COWBOY AND A LONG WAY FROM HOME ...
RIBBIT
THE END
BONHOMME 15

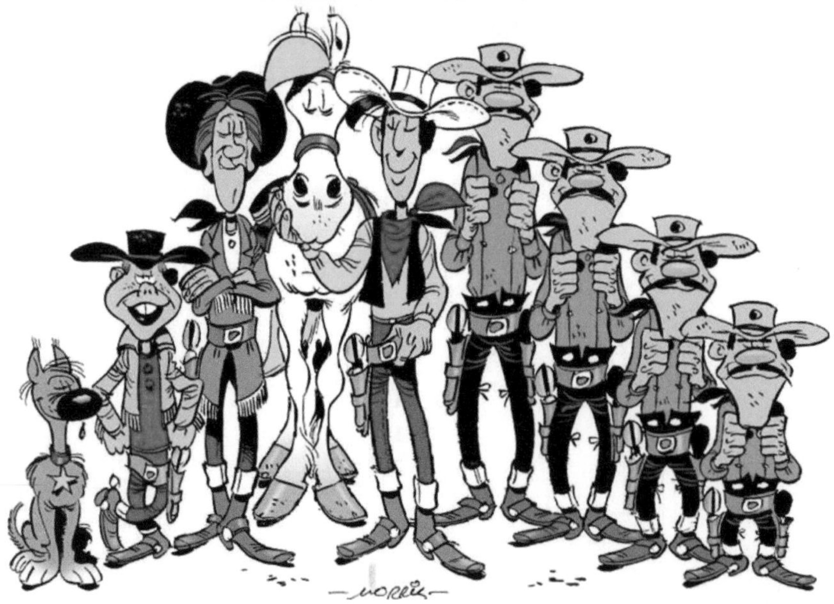
MORRIS

ALREADY AVAILABLE IN THE REGULAR SERIES

Lucky Luke 1 - Billy the Kid	Lucky Luke 41 - The Daily Star
Lucky Luke 2 - Ghost Town	Lucky Luke 42 - Lone Riders
Lucky Luke 3 - Dalton City	Lucky Luke 43 - The Bluefeet Are Coming!
Lucky Luke 4 - Jesse James	Lucky Luke 44 - Lucky Luke Versus Pat Poker
Lucky Luke 5 - In the Shadow of the Derricks	Lucky Luke 45 - Tying the Knot
Lucky Luke 6 - Ma Dalton	Lucky Luke 46 - The Pony Express
Lucky Luke 7 - Barbed Wire on the Prairie	Lucky Luke 47 - Outlaws
Lucky Luke 8 - Calamity Jane	Lucky Luke 48 - Dick Digger's Gold Mine
Lucky Luke 9 - The Wagon Train	Lucky Luke 49 - The Dalton's Amnesia
Lucky Luke 10 - Tortillas for the Daltons	Lucky Luke 50 - Seven Stories
Lucky Luke 11 - Western Circus	Lucky Luke 51 - The Painter
Lucky Luke 12 - The Rivals of Painful Gulch	Lucky Luke 52 - The Beautiful Province
Lucky Luke 13 - The Tenderfoot	Lucky Luke 53 - Nitroglycerin
Lucky Luke 14 - The Dashing White Cowboy	Lucky Luke 54 - Rodeo
Lucky Luke 15 - The Daltons in the Blizzard	Lucky Luke 55 - Arizona
Lucky Luke 16 - The Black Hills	Lucky Luke 56 - Under a Western Sky
Lucky Luke 17 - Apache Canyon	Lucky Luke 57 - Legends of the West
Lucky Luke 18 - The Escort	Lucky Luke 58 - The Daltons' Stash
Lucky Luke 19 - On the Daltons' Trail	Lucky Luke 59 - Bride of Lucky Luke
Lucky Luke 20 - The Oklahoma Land Rush	Lucky Luke 60 - The Ballad of the Daltons
Lucky Luke 21 - The 20th Cavalry	Lucky Luke 61 - Daisy Town
Lucky Luke 22 - Emperor Smith	Lucky Luke 62 - The Cursed Ranch
Lucky Luke 23 - A Cure for the Daltons	Lucky Luke 63 - Sarah Bernhardt
Lucky Luke 24 - The Judge	Lucky Luke 64 - The Wedding Crashers
Lucky Luke 25 - The Stagecoach	Lucky Luke 65 - Ghost Hunt
Lucky Luke 26 - The Bounty Hunter	Lucky Luke 66 - The Promised Land
Lucky Luke 27 - Lucky Luke Versus Joss Jamon	Lucky Luke 67 - Belle Starr
Lucky Luke 28 - The Dalton Cousins	Lucky Luke 68 - Bridge Over the Mississippi
Lucky Luke 29 - The Grand Duke	Lucky Luke 69 - Kid Lucky
Lucky Luke 30 - The Daltons' Escape	Lucky Luke 70 - O.K. Corral
Lucky Luke 31 - Lucky Luke Versus the Pinkertons	Lucky Luke 71 - A Cowboy in Paris
Lucky Luke 32 - Rails on the Prairie	Lucky Luke 72 - Marcel Dalton
Lucky Luke 33 - The One-Armed Bandit	Lucky Luke 73 - The Prophet
Lucky Luke 34 - The Daltons Always on the Run	Lucky Luke 74 - The Klondike
Lucky Luke 35 - The Singing Wire	Lucky Luke 75 - Rin Tin Can's Inheritance
Lucky Luke 36 - The Daltons Redeem Themselves	Lucky Luke 76 - Oklahoma Jim
Lucky Luke 37 - Fingers	Lucky Luke 77 - A Cowboy in High Cotton
Lucky Luke 38 - Doc Doxey's Elixir	Lucky Luke 78 - The Dalton Uncles
Lucky Luke 39 - The Man from Washington	Lucky Luke 79 - Steaming up the Mississippi
Lucky Luke 40 - Phil Wire	Lucky Luke 80 - The Alibi